MINI

TENERIFE

How to download your Free eBook

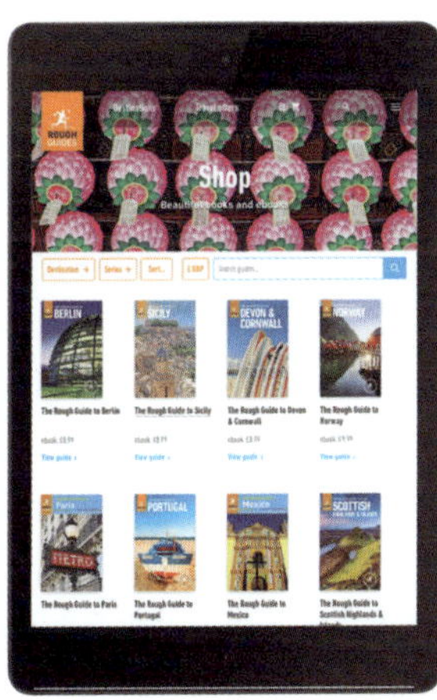

1. Visit **www.roughguides.com/free-ebook** or scan the **QR code** opposite

2. Enter the code **tenerife181**

3. Follow the simple step-by-step instructions

For troubleshooting contact: mail@roughguides.com

Samsonite

Contents

6 **Introduction**

- 14 10 Things not to miss
- 16 A perfect day in Tenerife
- 18 Foodie Tenerife
- 20 Cultural Tenerife

22 **History**

35 **Places**

- 35 The northeast
- 50 The north coast
- 61 El Teide
- 70 The northwest
- 78 The south

91 **Things to do**

- 91 Outdoor activities
- 95 Water activities
- 97 Spectator sports
- 98 Culture
- 99 Shopping
- 101 Nightlife
- 102 Festivals
- 105 Festivals and events

107 **Food and drink**

127 **Travel essentials**

142 **Index**

Introduction

Time signals on state radio and television in Spain give two times: one for mainland Spain and one for 'Las Canarias'. Cast adrift in the Atlantic Ocean over 1000km (620 miles) to the south of Spain and 115km (70 miles) from the west coast of Africa, Tenerife and the seven other official islands that make up the Canary archipelago don't see the sun rise until around one hour later than their mainland compatriots.

Sprawling across 2000 sq km (800 sq miles), Tenerife is the largest of these volcanic cones that began to erupt from the depths of the seabed more than twenty million years ago. Of the others, the three closest to Africa (Gran Canaria, Lanzarote and Fuerteventura) are the oldest, formed ten million years before Tenerife. Finally, some two million years after that, the Canaries' other western isles – La Palma, La Gomera and El Hierro – burst into life.

The beach at Puerto de la Cruz

Land of fire

On a clear day all the islands can be seen from the summit of Tenerife's Pico del Teide, which at 3718m (12,195ft), is the highest mountain in Spain. Its peak was created a million years ago inside the crater of a former, collapsed volcano, the

WHAT'S NEW

Over the past few years, Tenerife's gourmet dining scene has sky-rocketed: eight restaurants now hold ten of the much-coveted Michelin stars. The latest additions to this prestigious culinary rollcall were the Niki Pavanelli-helmed *Il Bocconcino by Royal Hideaway*, *Donaire* by Jesús Camacho at the *GF Victoria*, Víctor Suárez's *Haydée* at the *Gran Tacande*, all hotel restaurants in the Costa Adeje, and *Taste 1973* by Diego Schattenhofer at the *Europe Villa Cortés* in Playa de las Américas.

Did you know that Spain's first luxury hotel was right here in Tenerife? It opened more than 130 years ago near Puerto de la Cruz on the island's northern coast and was a favourite of crime writer Agatha Christie. The *Gran Hotel Taoro* closed around fifty years ago but after much renovation and refurbishment, the iconic hotel reopened in 2025 in all its former glory.

Circo de Cañadas, where the landscape is burnt and bleak. There has been no volcanic activity here for 500,000 years, though eruptions have occurred elsewhere on the island, the last in 1909 on Montaña Chinyero, near Santiago del Teide.

Lava fields are only part of a rich diversity of landscapes on Tenerife, the shape of an inverted triangle of just 2034 sq km (785 sq miles). It includes tropical gardens, misty forests, fertile mountain slopes, tranquil villages, rocky headlands and black beaches, the most popular of which have been lined with imported Sahara sand.

Balmy climes

The climate on Tenerife is pleasant all year round, with little variation in the average annual temperature of around 22°C (72°F) – one of the main reason the Canaries are such a popular destination. The Teide massif effectively splits Tenerife into two climatic zones, north and south.

The northerly trade winds whisk more cloud cover and rainfall to the north, with the coast enjoying a constant, warm, subtropical climate. Cloud conditions constantly vary, making it sometimes hard to know what to expect. Higher up, it is cooler and more humid, and the sun generally shines only in the mornings. Above the cloud layer the temperatures plummets at night; in winter the mercury drops below freezing and snow falls, creating small lakes as it melts.

The south of the island, where the popular tourist beaches have sprung up, is hot and dry, reaching almost desert conditions. Clouds are rare and there is little rainfall, but the sirocco wind from the south occasionally causes a sandy haze called the *calima*. A steady breeze on the south coast creates ideal windsurfing conditions.

Fine flora and curious critters

Climatic conditions and unusual geology have nurtured a rich variety of plants and wildlife, some of which are unique to the

WHEN TO GO

Thanks to the year-round balmy temperature, there's never a bad time to visit Tenerife. That said, the island has two high seasons in both summer and winter when resorts and beaches can get busy and crowded. Carnival comes to town each February, and hotels are booked up well in advance, so plan ahead if you're looking to join in the festivities. Spring can be a great time for hiking as temperatures tend to be slightly lower and the island's flora is starting to blossom. Autumn presents the ideal opportunity to explore the gourmet side of Tenerife, including visiting traditional *guachinches*. These casual pop-up restaurants only open for a few weeks after the wine harvest, when the vineyards sell unassuming Canarian food (grilled meat, stews, cheese) along with their own wine. Look out on roadsides in the north of the island for hand-painted signs directing you to local *guachinches*.

island. There are around 650 native species and nearly forty percent of the territory is under a conservation order. On Tenerife, four hundred of the two thousand naturally occurring plant species are endemic.

Bird of paradise is the Canaries' flower and a major export

Tenerife's extraordinary environment has attracted botanists down the centuries. From Germany came Alexander von Humboldt, who, in the nineteenth century, stopped on his way to South America and lavished fulsome praise on the islands. The French diplomat Sabin Berthelot, an enthusiast for all things Canarian, arrived on Tenerife in 1820 at the age of 26 and became director of the botanical gardens. From England in 1875 came Marianne North, whose works fill the gallery named after her at Kew Gardens in London.

What these experts discovered were tree-sized poinsettias, local variants of laurel and euphorbia, the *phoenix canariensis* palm and the legendary dragon tree (*dracaena draco*). Among an abundance of flowers that make the island particularly colourful in May and June are the red pillars of Teide echium or 'pride of Tenerife' (*orgullo de Tenerife*) and the pink-and-white Teide broom (*spartocytisus nubigens*), both of which thrive in the arid Cañadas.

The archipelago has thousands of insect species, though none is likely to cause you any harm. There are grasshoppers native to

Blue Teide finch, endemic to the Canaries

each island, and the ones on Tenerife grow to 12cm (5in). Its reptiles include the Canary species of lizard, skink and gecko.

The Canaries are also on one of the principal migration routes for whales: one-third of all species pass through local waters each year.

Rich birdlife

Many of the birds found on Tenerife will be familiar to Europeans, though there are unique ones to look out for, too. Most are shy, and though a variety of coloured doves have been spotted, don't expect to see many as you travel around. You might catch sight of the blue Teide finch in the national park. Forests of Canarian pines shelter the elusive blue chaffinch (endangered after the fires of July 2007 wiped out much of the island's pine forests) and the canary, a dull bird in the wild, which tragically becomes yellow and more boisterous when caged (or blinded, as they once were to make them sing louder).

In the scrubland you might see the Canarian pipit, barbary partridge or trumpeter finch. In the laurel and juniper forests, look out for the Canary Islands kinglet and native pigeons. Other unusual species include the collared pratincole, American golden plover, glossy ibis and barbary falcon. You will see ocean birds around the headlands or if you venture on boat trips, such as whale- or dolphin-watching.

A fragile ecology

The island's habitat is continually under pressure from the four million tourists who descend each year, making heavy demands on resources. Tree-felling, which began after the European conquest, has divested the island of lakes and rivers, and water is a precious commodity. Visitors should not be profligate with it. In addition, water treatment means that the taste isn't always great.

Ecology is on the mind of every islander, as ranks of new cement-block villas and apartments continue to mushroom across the landscape. Summer forest fires, too, have disastrous effects, often started by tourists' lack of care. In 2007, severe forest fires burnt more than a third of Tenerife's woodland and razed nine hundred homes. The Buenavista area and the Teno National Park were the worst affected. In 2012, blazes near Teide volcano ravaged large swaths of forest in the Santa Cruz

NOTES

The Canary Islands are one of the autonomous regions of Spain. Santa Cruz de Tenerife is the administrative capital of the western islands. The nearest island to Tenerife is La Gomera, 30km (18 miles) west. Gran Canaria, capital of the eastern isles, is 60km (36 miles) southeast, and the sea between them is 2000m (6560ft) deep.

SUSTAINABLE TRAVEL

Over the past few years, a debate has been simmering over the levels of tourism on the island and the impact vast numbers of visitors is having on resources, the environment and the community. That doesn't mean that Tenerife is anti-tourism – far from it. However, travellers are reminded to be responsible when it comes to things such as water usage – a scarce resource. Nearly half the island is protected natural space and following a spate of forest fires over recent years, people should pay extra attention to the safe disposal of litter and particularly cigarette ends when enjoying the many hiking trails. In fact, swerving the busy resorts in favour of lesser-trodden paths is encouraged, particularly the green north that is often overlooked. Whale-watching trips are popular but opt for responsible providers such as Biosean (www.biosean.com) or Blue Jack Sail (www.bluejacksail.com). Other ways to support the economy include visiting local cheesemakers such as family-run Quesería Montesdeoca (www.quesosmontesdeoca.com) and vineyards like Bodegas Ferrera (www.bodegasferrera.com), plus the many artisanal markets that pop up weekly across the island.

province, and in 2019, 50m (165ft) -high flames soared into the air, causing the evacuation of eight thousand people. Two years later, a fire in Arico affected over 3000 hectares (7400 acres) of forest area.

A fiery people

The population, including about 236,000 foreign-born residents, is around 966,000, with more than half living in the conurbation of Santa Cruz. *Tinerfeños* are often cheerful, gregarious and courteous, with a love of children, parties and football. According to a folk song, 'Canarians are like the giant Teide, quiet as snow on the outside and fire in the heart'. Their carnival is, after all, one of the greatest in the world.

NOTES

The native island dog is the Verdino. Smooth-haired and powerful, it weighs 40–50kg (90–110lb) and its name is a nod to its slightly greenish fur. There is a theory that the Canaries were named after the native canines (*canes* in Latin) found here in classical times.

The local Spanish accent is halfway between Madrid and Mexico. The 'c' and 'z' are not a lisped *th* as they are on the mainland, and consonants at the end of words sometimes fall away (examples include Santa Cru', La' Palma' and Juá'). Some words originate directly from South America (*guagua* for a bus), others from the colonial past.

Tourism is the main occupation of the islanders today. Agriculture is on the wane and some of the more remote villages have become abandoned. Since the conquest the island has absorbed a string of monocultures, from sugar to bananas and cochineal. Bananas are still one of the main crops grown, along with tomatoes and cut flowers, particularly the striking bird of paradise (*strelitzia*).

There are no mineral resources on the island, and no industry. As produce and manufactured goods have to be shipped in, the cost of living tends to be higher than in mainland Spain.

Traditional dress

10 Things not to miss

1

2

3

4

5

6

1 **LA OROTAVA**
La Orotava's Casa de los Balcones is a beautiful example of a traditional town mansion. See page 55.

2 **MASCA**
A dramatically located mountain village with a challenging hike down to the sea. See page 75.

3 **EL TEIDE**
This mighty volcano is Spain's highest mountain. See page 61.

4 **CASTILLO DE SAN MIGUEL**
The squat ancient castle in Garachico has fine views out to sea. See page 72.

5 **SAN CRISTÓBAL DE LA LAGUNA**
With its jumble of lovely old buildings, the former capital of Tenerife is a UNESCO World Heritage Site. See page 45.

6 **FORESTAL PARK TENERIFE**
Walk and zipline your way through the sky-high Canarian pine trees in this natural park, 1400m (1200ft) above sea level. See page 92.

7 **MUSEO DE LA NATURALEZA Y ARQUEOLOGÍA**
Located in Santa Cruz, this excellent nature and archaeology museum is Tenerife's largest. See page 40.

8 **LOS GIGANTES**
A hub for diving and boat trips, Los Gigantes is huddled at the foot of the sheer cliffs that give the resort its name. See page 77.

9 **WHALE-WATCHING**
Spotting pilot whales and bottle-nosed dolphins between Tenerife and La Gomera is an unforgettable experience. See page 96.

10 **PARQUE ETNOGRÁFICO PIRÁMIDES DE GÜÍMAR**
These structures are thought to be pyramids built for sun worship. See page 87.

A perfect day in Tenerife

9AM

Breakfast. For a relaxing start to the morning, soak up the views over the beach, port and promenade at Playa de los Cristianos, while breakfasting on delicious coffee and freshly baked pastries at *Gran Cafè Tenerife* (Av. Los Playeros 45).

10AM

Adeje. Drive north on the main TF1 road then divert to the unspoilt hill town of Adeje, former seat of an Indigenous Guanche community and later stronghold of the Counts of Gomera. Visit the remains of Casa Fuerte and amble along the steep Rambla, flanked by pavement bars and cafés. Adeje is the entry point to the Barranco del Infierno (Hell's Gorge), a popular 4-mile (6.3km) return hike, which should be saved for another day.

11.30AM

Arguayo. Rejoin the main road wending north. After Chio head right via the village of Arguayo, home to the Centro Alfarero y Museo Etnográfico Cha Domitila (Calle Ctra. General 35), where you can watch potters at work and purchase traditional ceramics.

12.30PM

Masca. Continue north via Las Manchas to Santiago del Teide. From here press on to Tenerife's most picturesque village – Masca, poised at the head of a dramatic gorge. Enjoy the breathtaking views from one of the roadside restaurants – *El Guanche* (C. El Lomito, s/n) is a good bet for traditional cuisine.

2PM

Garachico. Return to the main road and drive north (TF-82) to the charming coastal village of Garachico. Spend a couple of hours here, taking a cooling dip in the lava rock pools, visiting the ex-Convent of San Francisco, admiring the views from Castillo de San Miguel and lingering over a drink in the plaza.

4PM

West coast. Head back south on the main road, then at Tamaimo turn on to the TF454 for Los Gigantes. 'The Giants' is named after the soaring volcanic walls that plummet into the sea. Continue along the coast, pausing at the fishing village and beach resort of Playa de San Juan.

7PM

Sunset wining and dining. Enjoy a cocktail at *La Caleta* on the Costa Adeje, then tuck into freshly caught seafood at *Restaurante Celso* (www.restaurantecelso.com) or *Masía del Mar* (www.masiadelmargroup.com), served with stunning views over the Atlantic Ocean.

11PM

Nightlife. End the evening at the *Papagayo Beach Club* (www.papagayobeachclub.com) in Playa de las Américas, watching the sun sink low before partying on a packed dancefloor.

Foodie Tenerife

9.30AM

Breakfast. Kick off the day with a dash of *Tinerfeño* rocket fuel at *Café Palmelita* (www.palmelita.es) in Santa Cruz. Order a *barraquito* – a traditional coffee consisting of condensed milk, Licor 43, espresso, hot milk, foam, a dusting of cinnamon and a twist of lemon peel.

10.15AM

Make for the market. Walk up Calle del Castillo and turn left at Calle Valentín Sanz, head over the bridge and directly ahead you'll spot La Recova, a local market that's been serving up fresh produce to shoppers since 1943. Browse for gourmand souvenirs such as honey rum and taste local cheeses and fruits.

11.30AM

Go bananas. Jump in the car and head north on the TF-5 to El Rincón to the BananaECOPlantation (www.bananaecoplantation.com) for a tour around the banana plants and to learn about the history and importance of the fruit for the Tenerife economy – and, of course, taste some delectable banana products.

2PM

Lunch. Head along the coast on the TF-5 to Santa Ursula to *El Calderito de la Abuela* (www.elcalderitodelaabuela.net). Famed in these parts for its classic Canarian cuisine, the glass-fronted restaurant prides itself on quality ingredients – and fine views. Try to snag a table at the window for stunning vistas over nearby Puerto de la Cruz.

4PM

Wine tasting. Take the motorway to El Sauzal to the Casa del Vino de Tenerife (www.casadelvinotenerife.com). This seventeenth-century *hacienda* houses a wine museum and restaurant, but book onto one of its tasting sessions to learn about (and sample) wines made from indigenous grape varieties such as Malvasía and Listán Negro.

6PM

La Laguna. Make your way back to the capital, stopping en route to stroll the historic streets of La Laguna. Grab a coffee or aperitivo at one of the many cafés or perhaps in the charming interior patio of *La Laguna Gran Hotel* (www.lalagunagranhotel.com).

8PM

Tasting table. The tiny restaurant of *Colmado 1917* (www.colmado1917.com) in the *Grand Mencey* hotel has just ten seats. Its tasting menu champions seasonal, local cuisine with minimal intervention, paired with wines from the island.

11PM

La Noria. Wander through the city to the old town and Calle la Noria. By day this street is one of the quietest in the capital, but at night it comes alive with the coolest bars and restaurants.

Cultural Tenerife

9AM

Street art in Puerto de la Cruz. Grab a latte from *Slow Coffee Tenerife* (www.slowcoffeetenerife.com) and strike out in search of street art; at least fifteen pieces are dotted around Puerto de la Cruz. The city hosts the annual International Street Art Festival, Mueca, each May.

11.30AM

La Orotava. Jump on bus 351 for the fifteen-minute journey to this grand town – once home to the island's wealthy, whose legacy lingers on in the handsome buildings and showy squares.

12.30PM

Casa de los Balcones. Stop by the intriguing Casa de los Balcones, with its extraordinary Canarian pinewood balconies, and see the main square that gets covered in a giant flower and sand mural each Corpus Christi in May and June.

2PM

Lunch. Catch bus 108 towards La Laguna. Fuel your sightseeing efforts with the innovative fusion plates at *Restaurante Guaydil* (www.restauranteguaydil.com); try the blue cheese and banana *croquetas*.

3PM

City tour. Walk off lunch around the historic streets of the old capital city. The local council organises free guided tours on request or provides self-guided routes. The street plan here was used as the blueprint for Havana in Cuba.

5.30PM

Santa Cruz. Hop on the tram that runs all the way to Santa Cruz. While it might be the 'new' capital, there's plenty to see and do, such as the Museum of Nature and Archaeology (MUNA; www.museosdetenerife.org/muna-museo-de-naturaleza-y-arqueologia), where you'll learn about the *guanches* – the island's original inhabitants. Pop next door to the TEA Tenerife Espacio de las Artes (https://teatenerife.es), the contemporary art gallery, for something completely different.

7PM

Dinner. Feast on tapas and wine at *Gastrobar Cortxo* (Plaza de Ireneo Gonzalez 5), a lovely little haunt with a huge list of bottles, including a fine selection of local labels. Though there are very few seats inside, the place to be is on the terrace outside, watching the action unfold in the pretty square.

8PM

El Auditorio. Walk down to the gravity-defying Auditorio de Tenerife Adán Martín opera house to catch a show or concert, or simply marvel at the architectural genius of Santiago Calatrava. Grab a drink at *La Ventita* (Padre Moore 4) before catching a bus back to Puerto – they run until late.

History

La Orotava Valley behind Puerto de la Cruz on the north coast of Tenerife is the most fertile part of the island. When the island's Hispanic conquerors arrived in the fifteenth century, they found the Taoro living here, the richest of nine island communities, whose chief or *mencey* was called Tanasú. These tall, athletic people called Guanches somehow reached the Canary Islands in the first or second century BC from Northwest Africa, and were related to the Imazighen (Berbers). They developed a written language, which remains largely undeciphered, and were ruled through councils called *tagorors*, with their court in Adeje on the west coast.

Moss furring an ancient Guanche pot

The island provided natural shelter with many caves (still used today in Chinameda and Fasnia), which they decorated; they built stone huts, too.

NOTES

The Guanches were related to the Imazighen (Berbers) of North Africa, though how they reached the Canary Islands from Africa is a mystery. The Romans arrived to find that the islanders did not possess boats.

Guanche culture

Not surprisingly, the volcanic giant of El Teide was central to worship for the Guanches. Their culture can be glimpsed through their funerary rites, and particularly their mummifying rituals, which are explained at the Museo de Naturaleza y Arqueología in Santa Cruz. They likely worshipped the sun, and the ancient 'pyramids' that the Norwegian explorer Thor Heyerdahl discovered in 1990 in Güímar are convincing evidence of how their sacred sites may have looked (though Spanish archaeologists believe the pyramids were built in nineteenth century).

The Guanches created no boats, nor did the wheel occur to them, but they were adept potters, making their finest vessels for religious purposes and storing grain. Pottery and cultivation were traditionally women's work. Men hunted and tended the animals. A lack of metal ore on the island left the Guanches stuck in the Stone Age, with blunt instruments sharpened by bones and black volcanic obsidian, found in the Cañadas.

For food, they hunted wild cats and pigs, Barbary partridges and quail. They also kept pigs, sheep and, principally, goats, whose skins provided the material of the garments they wore. But it was as a land of canines that the island group may have been given its name. In the first century AD, Pliny wrote of an expedition to the archipelago by King Juba II of Mauretania, who apparently saw many dogs roaming there. *Canis* is the Latin for dog, hence Canary Islands. The islands were fixed on the earliest classical maps as the

'Insulae Fortunatae', the Fortunate Islands, and were then the westernmost point of the known world.

The conquest

Spanish cartographers properly mapped the islands at the end of the fourteenth century when the name Tenerife appeared for the first time, although it is thought that it comes from the native '*teni iru*', meaning snowy peak. The Genoese Lanzarotto Malocello is generally thought to have led the first European expedition to the Canaries, landing in the 1330s on the island that bears his name. Within a few decades, conquest of the archipelago had begun. Jean de Béthencourt, a Norman navigator employed by

Illustration of a priest christening a Guanche

Henri III of Castile, made the initial advances, seizing the eastern isles and then, in 1405, El Hierro, the smallest of the western isles. Tenerife, the most populous of the islands, was still in Guanche hands in 1492 when Christopher Columbus docked at neighbouring Gran Canaria and La Gomera on his voyage to the Americas (noting, as he did so, an eruption of El Teide, and recording that his crew thought it a sign that they should turn back).

Statue of a Guanche King in Candelaria

Missionaries and conquerors

That same year, Alfonso Fernandez de Lugo, a mercenary backed by Genoese merchants, seized La Palma, following a six-year campaign against Gran Canaria. Only Tenerife remained in native hands. On the coast of Tenerife, De Lugo easily defeated local communities, moving to the better-defended interior. However, he was caught in a trap at Barranco de Acentejo (now the town of La Matanza, 'The Slaughter'), 16km (10 miles) into the Orotava Valley by Taoro chief Bencomo.

De Lugo escaped, only to return to the island with a larger force the following year and win a decisive victory on the plains of La Vitoria de Acentejo, a couple of miles south of his earlier defeat. Some two thousand Guanches were massacred by the sophisticated Spanish crossbow, and Bentor, the last chief of the Taoro, died by suicide.

De Lugo established his capital at San Cristóbal de la Laguna in the middle of the fertile Valle de Aguere, within striking distance of both the north and east coasts. The statue of Jesus that he had carted to the island came to rest here in the Santuario del Cristo, and the flag that had claimed Tenerife for Spain was subsequently hung in the town hall. Santa Iglesia cathedral, which was founded ten years later in 1515, became De Lugo's resting place.

The effect of the conquerors on the local population was disastrous. The new diseases they brought spread among the Guanche population, and many were forced into slavery. From the thousands that had inhabited the island, soon only a few hundred remained. The investors in De Lugo's expedition were rewarded with plots of land in the west, where sugar cane was introduced for the refineries built at Realejos and Icod. De Lugo continued to seek Italian finance to fuel the new economy, and Portuguese workers were imported to harvest the canes on a share-cropping basis.

Sugar and wine

The landscape began to change, too. Mills were stoked with timber cut from the forests, which had the long-term effect of reducing rainfall and drying up lakes, streams and springs.

Canarian sugar could not compete with that being planted in the Americas, so by the end of the fifteenth century, vineyards of the Malvasía grape had been planted on the north of the island instead, and it was wine that offered an alternative economy as the sugar trade slumped. The grape produced sweet, dessert wines that travelled well and were particularly

NOTES

It's said that the illicit trade of Canarian wine, particularly the much-prized sweet Malvasía (Malmsey) was used by Benjamin Franklin and Robert Morris to fund the American War of Independence (1775–83).

Admiral Nelson, wounded at Tenerife in 1797

enjoyed by Northern Europeans. By the time Shakespeare's Falstaff and Sir Toby Belch were downing 'cups of Canary', and Bostonians were talking of 'the Isles of Wine', it had become the principal export.

The Canary Islands were located on the trade route to the 'New World', thus ships regularly called by Tenerife's excellent harbours, principally Garachico on the north coast, carrying sugar and likely slaves. Trade between Spain and the Americas was confined to Spanish nationals, so smuggling and piracy became part of daily life. But in 1610 the Spanish government relaxed this restriction, and foreign capitalists hotfooted to Tenerife. By the mid-century, the island had 1500 English and Dutch residents out of a population of 50,000.

The Malvasía grape's rival was Madeira, from the Portuguese island of the same name, and when England sided with Portugal in the War of the Spanish Succession (1701–14) a major market was lost. However, Tenerife remained the archipelago's major wine producer for another century, and the wealth it created paid for the rich architecture of wine towns such as Orotava. In 1706, when a volcanic eruption devastated Garachico, Puerto de la Cruz became the island's main port.

A university was founded in La Laguna at the start of the eighteenth century and an intelligentsia flourished among the 70,000 *Tinerfeños*. But prosperity did not survive the century, and the wine trade floundered. Global conflict, with America's War of Independence (1775–83) and the Napoleonic wars, during which Admiral Nelson blockaded Santa Cruz, was harmful to trade. Hardship was compounded by revolutions in Latin America, where many Canarians had fled to seek their fortunes, and payments to the families left behind were disrupted.

Beetles to bananas

After the wine trade slumped, the cochineal beetle was introduced from Mexico, mainly in the eastern isles. This had a brutalising effect on the landscape as native trees were replaced by cacti for the critter to feed on. The crop plummeted into decline when synthetic dyes were developed in the late nineteenth century, by which time bananas were making money.

In 1822 Santa Cruz had become the official capital of the archipelago and thirty years later each island was granted free trade status for one of its ports. Tenerife, unusually, had two: Puerto de la Cruz and Santa Cruz, which then had the

NOTES

Secundino Delgado was the most influential independence figure. He went to work in Cuba at 14, but it was in Venezuela, in 1897, that he founded *El Guanche*, a newspaper calling for independence in the Canary Islands.

Lope Félix de Vega was a key figure in the Spanish Golden Age of Baroque literature

archipelago's only first-class road, to La Orotava. Tenerife's superiority took a knock in 1881, though, when a harbour improvement scheme for Las Palmas on Gran Canaria eclipsed Santa Cruz.

A profound change began to take root in the later part of the nineteenth century, when refrigeration arrived. Tourists also travelled to the island on fruit boats along with this new technology. The huge and extremely opulent *Gran Hotel Taoro* in Puerto de la Cruz was built in 1892 to cater specifically for such visitors, and for many years it was the largest hotel in Spain.

The Spanish Civil War

The Spanish Second Republic of 1931 sparked new hopes of autonomy, but General Franco's uprising of 1936 put paid to any such aspirations for more than forty years. Suspected of concocting plans against the Republican government, Franco had been banished to Tenerife in March to keep him out of the way. From Las Palmas, however, he flew to the Spanish North African enclave of Melilla on 18 July. Two days later the uprising that led to the civil war was underway and the islands were in Franco's hands – La Palma was shelled by the navy before being overcome. On Tenerife, Lt Gonzales Campos was the only officer to oppose the uprising, and he was summarily shot, along with the civil governor. Republican prisoners and suspects were herded into Fyffes' banana warehouse, near Santa Cruz football ground, and shot in batches. An ally of Hitler and Mussolini, Franco was ostracised by

Illustration of Las Palmas de Gran Canaria

the rest of the world until the early 1950s when Spain was welcomed back into the international community in exchange for accepting NATO bases.

Tourism and the post-Franco years

After the death of Franco in 1975, King Juan Carlos restored a system of democracy. Three years later a new Constitution granted degrees of autonomy to the country's regions, including the Canary Islands.

Tourism had already begun with a vengeance in Tenerife, after direct flights to the island started in 1959. Pressure on Puerto de la Cruz to build more hotels caused people within the area to sell up and transfer their plantations to the dry south, piping water into the region and opening up the barren lands in Adeje and Arona. On this coast, tourists in search of a tan flocked to the port of Los Cristianos. This is where the boom really exploded, sprawling up into Playa de las Américas, which was created in 1978, the same year that the nearby airport of Reina Sofia opened. Resorts continue to mushroom along the coast, boosting the island's economy.

Nowadays, most tourists beeline for these resorts, which are renowned for cheap package breaks and raucous nightlife. However, an increasing number of visitors are discovering the greener, quieter and more traditional Tenerife of the north. A growing crop of hotels here, many in rustic or local Canarian style, are luring those who want to venture off the beaten track. On the island as a whole, new or refurbished luxury and boutique hotels, year-round golf, chic nightlife, whale-watching, cycling, trekking and the opening of gourmet restaurants are successfully working to change the long-held image of a downmarket 'sun, sea and sand' destination. Thanks to major developments in the gastronomic scene, outdoor adventure and stargazing, Tenerife is emerging as go-to for cultural, active and alternative holidays.

Chronology

c. 3000BC Settlers arrive from Africa.

206BC Guanches reach the island.

1st century AD Classical writers describe the islands on the edge of the known world populated by dogs (*canis*, hence Canaries).

1st–13th centuries Guanche society develops under chief leadership.

1492 Christopher Columbus witnesses eruption of Mount Teide en route to the Americas.

1495 Bencor, the last chief of the Taoro, dies by suicide when Tenerife is conquered by Alfonso Fernandez de Lugo at the Battle of Acentejo.

University of La Laguna

1701–14 The Canaries' university founded in La Laguna.
1706 Mount Teide erupts, destroying the main port of Garachico.
1797 Admiral Nelson's attack on Santa Cruz repelled.
1850–1900 Large-scale emigration to Latin America.
1880s Bananas introduced.
1936 General Franco launches his rebellion from Tenerife.
1959 First direct flights to Tenerife bring a new wave of tourists.
1978 The Canaries become autonomous within Spain.
1986 Spain joins the EU and negotiates a special status for the Canaries.
1995 Canary Islands integrated into the EU but retain important tax privileges.
1999 The euro replaces the peseta as the currency of Spain.
2006 Sharp rise in the number of immigrants from Africa.
2007 Severe forest fires ravage the west of the island.
2010 Teide National Park provides a backdrop for the film version of *Clash of the Titans* and two years later for its sequel *Wrath of the Titans*.
2012 Blazes destroy large swathes of forest in the Santa Cruz province.
2015 Regional elections in the Canary Islands are won by the Coalición Canaria (CC), which forms a coalition cabinet with the Partido Socialista Canario (PSOE).
2017 Cabinet reshuffle after PSOE ministers leave the government.
2019 Canarian regional election won by PSOE.
2020 Coronavirus pandemic spreads to Canary Islands.
2021 Forest fire in Arico municipality razes over 3000 hectares (7500 acres) of land.
2024 Protests decry mass tourism and criticise the island government's tourism strategy.
2025 The Michelin Guide awards stars to two more restaurants, bringing the island's combined total to ten stars.
2025 Reopening of *Gran Hotel Taoro*, Spain's first large luxury hotel in Spain when it originally launched in 1890.

Playa de las Teresitas, with Santa Cruz in the distance

Places

Tenerife is not large and as a result, it is easy to make forays from any base. Nowhere is far away, and it is possible to hire a car and drive from the coast to El Teide, scale its summit, and pick up handmade artisanal goods at La Orotava on the way back– all in a morning.

For much of the island, however, you don't need a car. Buses are regular and inexpensive. From the capital, Santa Cruz de Tenerife, you can have a day out on the opposite coast in Puerto de la Cruz, stopping off at the UNESCO World Heritage Site of San Cristóbal de La Laguna, with enough time to enjoy both places at an unhurried pace and return later in the day. You can also make day-trips to these places from Los Cristianos and Playa de las Américas in the south.

The route that follows starts in Santa Cruz and continues anticlockwise around the island.

The northeast

Highlights

- **Santa Cruz de Tenerife**, see page 35
- **San Cristóbal La Laguna**, see page 45
- **The Anaga Hills**, see page 47

Santa Cruz de Tenerife

Tenerife's capital, principal port and most vibrant town is on the northeastern arm of the island, facing southwest and looking towards Gran Canaria, an hour's jet-foil ferry trip away. **Santa Cruz de Tenerife** ❶ doesn't have a core municipal or cathedral square; instead the main action unfurls on the pedestrianised streets and squares leading up from the port, and on the Rambla that sweeps round the top of the town. Good for shops, restaurants and nightlife, Santa Cruz is also the cultural hub of Tenerife.

The sprawling waterfront area reaches its apex at **Plaza de España** Ⓐ; to the southwest are the container ports and the industrial zone, to the northeast the jacaranda-lined Avenida de Anaga passes beside the ferry port and yachting harbour. The square underwent a complete transformation several years ago by the innovative Swiss architects Herzog and de Meuron. The focal point is a huge, circular wading pool with a centrepiece geyser-like fountain, shaded by trees. The former heart of the square, the **Monumento a los Caídos**, dedicated to the fallen nationalists in the Civil War, was integrated into the design.

The Cabildo Insular and post office on Plaza de España

WHERE TO SHOOT THE BEST PICTURES

You'll find photo opportunities all over Tenerife, and often the best spots will be those that you just stumble upon as you travel around the island. There are also countless *miradores* (viewing points) from which you are guaranteed good vistas. That said, if you're looking for pictures of some of the main sights, there are some classic and quirky places to set up your camera. For views of El Teide, head to Mirador Azulejos II where you'll be able to give context to the peak, with volcanic scenery and the gaze-focusing road all in the shot. Alternatively, frame the mountain at La Ventana de Igueque, a natural rock window with a perfect view of El Teide. Túnel de las Hadas (Fairy Tunnel) in Parque Rural de Anaga is a popular spot as the misty forest is framed by harshly cut rock. In the south, try La Caleta for views of La Gomera, or Playa Montaña Amarilla for its interesting golden rock formations. La Laguna's historic streets are all photogenic, but to capture the essence of the city, face up Calle Obispo Rey Redondo to put the church belltower centre stage, while the eyeline is guided by the cobbled street and handsome buildings.

The Art Deco buildings at the southern end of the square are the post-office headquarters, the **Cabildo Insular**, containing government offices and the main tourist office.

Shopping area

Running up from the Plaza de España is **Plaza de la Candelaria**, where a statue of the island's patron dates from 1772. This is the start of the main pedestrianised area, and the pavement cafés are a popular meeting place. **Calle del Castillo** ❸, the principal shopping street, sweeps inland past the **Parlamento de Canarias** (guided tours usually take place every Sat 10am–1pm), on the right. The 1898 Neoclassical edifice, designed by Antonio Pintor, has been augmented to include the buildings fronting Castillo, with a green metal construction on its upper floors. Calle del

Castillo ends at **Plaza Weyler**, where the white marble *La Fuente* (*The Fountain*) by Achille Canessa is overlooked by the Capitanía General, the islands' military headquarters. This is where Franco was stationed when he started the Civil War.

On the north side of Calle del Castillo is the **Plaza del Príncipe de Asturias**, one of the city's most pleasant squares. On the plaza's southeast side, near the Circulo de Amistad, is the **Museo de Bellas Artes** Ⓒ (free), whose facade is adorned with busts of poets, philosophers and musicians. Inside is a library and, on the first and second floors, a gallery of sixteenth- to twentieth-century paintings. These include a panoramic picture of the foundation of Santa Cruz by Alonso de Lugo in 1494, two years after he had seized the island, and among portraits of local aristocracy is one of the French consul and botanist Sabin Berthelot, who did so much for Tenerife's plant life.

Behind the museum is the **Iglesia de San Francisco de Asís**, founded in 1680 and part of a former convent where concerts sometimes take place.

The oldest church

Eight years after Santa Cruz was founded, the town's first chapel was built where the city's main church, **Iglesia Matriz de Nuestra Señora de la Concepción** Ⓓ, stands today, just to the southwest of the Cabildo Insular. The cross that De Lugo brought ashore is among its treasures. In 1652 the church was rebuilt after a fire, its octagonal tower acting as a lookout point. The lovely balcony on its exterior – a feature of church architecture throughout the island

NOTES

Santa Cruz entered the *Guinness World Records* when an unprecedented crowd of a quarter of a million filled the Plaza de España for the 1987 carnival. The Tenerife carnival is one of the biggest in Europe.

The facade of the Teatro Guimerá

– gives its southwest front a domestic appearance. Inside, the space is cool and impressive, and the beautiful coffered *mudéjar*-style ceiling is also a typical design flourish.

In the streets around the church are some of the oldest buildings in Santa Cruz, many attractively maintained in warm, earthy hues. Stop for a glass of local wine in La Concepción, a district that comes alive after dark, its cafés and bars bustling until the early hours. Where Calle Dominguez Alfonso meets Puente General Serrador, there is a small square that often hosts evening concerts.

If you are strolling here at night, you may be lucky to chance on street theatre where the actors use the doors and balconies of the houses in their performances. Nearby, the **Teatro Guimerá** (www.teatroguimera.es) was named after the playwright Ángel Guimerá, who was born in Santa Cruz in 1849 and made his name

GENTLEMEN AT WAR

In 1797 Admiral Nelson attacked Santa Cruz. Leading the night assault, he leapt ashore only to have his right elbow shattered by grapeshot from a cannon in the Castillo de Paso Alto. The ambush was a failure, but the Spanish Governor sent each captured man back to his ship with a bottle of wine and a loaf of bread. His arm amputated, Nelson returned the compliment by sending the governor cheese and a cask of beer. The captured British flags are stored in a glass case in Nuestra Señora de le Concepción church.

in Barcelona with *Terra Baixa* in 1896. It also stages concerts and dance performances. Not far, on Calle Clavel 10, is yet another cultural centre – **Equipo Para** (www.equipopara.org) – a meeting place for artists and intellectuals as well as a concert, workshop and exhibition venue with the benefit of a small bar.

Across the Barranco

From Nuestra Señora de la Concepción, a bridge crosses a *barranco* (dry riverbed) to the former town hospital, now the **Museo de la Naturaleza y Arqueología** **E** (www.museosdetenerife.org; charge). As the name implies, all island life is represented here, and this is a good starting point for understanding Tenerife's geographical and historical aspects. Spread across three floors around two courtyards, it swarms with schoolchildren in term-time but is large enough to feel peaceful even at its busiest. The island's flora and fauna are fully explained, as is its geology, with descriptions of winds, currents and volcanoes. Humans feature early on, with mummified Guanches, and displays show how the Indigenous population lived. At the end is a café and an excellent bookshop.

Just west of the museum, the **TEA Tenerife Espacio de las Artes** **F** (www.teatenerife.es; free), designed by Swiss architect duo Herzog and de Meuron, is the cultural heart of the city. It houses numerous exhibition halls, the Tenerife Island Photography Centre and a splendid library. Nearby, on Plaza Santa Cruz de la Sierra, the **Mercado de Nuestra Señora de África** Ⓖ, popularly known as **La Recova** (www.la-recova.com) is a vibrant morning market that showcases the bounty of the island. Spread across two floors, stalls are piled high with colourful flowers, aromatic herbs, fruit, vegetables, meat and fish. On Sunday mornings there is a flea market, and stalls tumble down Calle José Manuel Guimerá.

Auditorio and Parque Marítimo

Calle José Manuel Guimerá leads down to the main highway, Avenida Tres de Mayo, which connects the docks to the Autopista

The Auditorio, home of the Tenerife Symphony Orchestra

Playa de Benijo

del Norte, while the Avenida de la Constitución continues past the port towards the Autopista del Sur. The latter has become the focus of post-millennium developments with the elegant **Auditorio de Tenerife Adán Martín** or **El Auditorio** (www.auditoriodetenerife.com), a concert hall built in 2003 by Valencian architect Santiago Calatrava. It is home to the Tenerife Symphony Orchestra. Beside it is a bus station, and just behind, beyond the old Castillo San Juan, the **Parque Marítimo César Manrique** H (https://parquemaritimosantacruz.es; charge) is a breezy area of azure seawater pools designed by the Lanzarote artist César Manrique (see page 53), with trees, flowers and waterfalls. There's a café and restaurant, and a day out here is as good as at the beach. Adjacent, a **Palmetum** (http://palmetumtenerife.es; charge) brims with palm trees from all over the world.

The Rambla

Santa Cruz's other main avenue, the **Rambla**, meanders around the back of the town and arrives at the Avenida de Anaga, by the waterfront next to the **Museo Militar Regional de Canarias** (free). This contains some of the armour worn by the Spanish conquerors, souvenirs from Nelson's attack, including El Tigre, the cannon that shattered his right elbow (see box), and the background to Franco's uprising in 1936. The Rambla's central pedestrian walkway, under jacaranda and Judas trees, makes it ideal for the evening *paseo* (stroll). Outdoor sculpture exhibitions have been held here since the 1970s and Henry Moore's *Goslar Warrior* is among a number of works that remain. The Rambla also passes the *Grand Mencey Hotel*, which has hosted everyone from monarchs to Hollywood royalty – although its guestbook is strictly confidential. A walk down the Rambla will also take you past the city's largest park, the 6-hectare (15-acre) **Parque García Sanabria ❶**, which has exotic plants and a pleasant café. A Swiss-made *reloj de flores* (flower clock), situated by the entrance near Calle Pilar, is one of *Santacruceros'* favourite meeting points.

The city's beach

Avenida de Anaga wiggles north, tracing the coast past the yacht clubs, then towards the town's summer playground, **Playa de las Teresitas ❷** (served by bus 910, which runs the 7km/4 miles along the waterfront every ten to twenty minutes). It is the most golden beach on the island, its imported Sahara sand lapped by shallow waters. Dogs, surfboards, ball games and the hanging of towels or clothes on trees are all banned. Kiosks sell snacks, and at weekends locals enliven the atmosphere at the restaurants, notably the *Cofradía de Pescadores* by the fishermen's shacks. There are more places to eat in **San Andrés ❸**, the fishing village of the original port just outside Santa Cruz, where the road heads into the Anaga Hills. After fifteen minutes' drive, the road reaches the **Mirador de**

Rosa Sosa, offering a final, stunning glimpse of the coast as well as walks through glorious, herb-scented hills.

On the coast beyond Playa de las Teresitas the road winds without let-up; the only exception is the **Punta de los Organos** *mirador*, which provides a last chance to look down on the beach. A couple of kilometres further on, a turn leads down to the secluded beach of Las Gaviotas beneath the cliffs, where swimsuits are optional. The road ends at **Igueste**, an attractive huddle of white villas among terraces of mangoes and avocados, wiggling steeply down before coming to a stop several hundred metres short of a small grey beach. From here you can walk to the little beach and one-family hamlet of **Antequera**.

Carved balcony in La Laguna

San Cristóbal La Laguna

Designated the capital of Tenerife by the island's conqueror, Alonso de Lugo, **San Cristóbal de la Laguna** ❹ is visibly the most ancient town on the island, with mansions dating from the fifteenth century. It is generally known simply as La Laguna, but the lagoon on which it once stood and named after has long since disappeared. The town, a UNESCO World Heritage Site, is at the heart of a large agricultural district, and is a centre of learning and religion, with a university and bishop's see.

While only a twenty-minute journey from Santa Cruz, the climate is noticeably cooler in La Laguna. The old part of town, the *casco histórico*, is on a grid system, and the starting point of a visit should be the **Plaza del Adelantado**. The municipal market once held at the far end of the square has been rehoused on Plaza del Cristo, ten minutes' walk away. The town is popular with visitors from the capital on weekends, when parking is difficult and the square's bars are buzzing. On the opposite side of the plaza are a trio of impressive but disparate buildings. To the left, the Neoclassical **Ayuntamiento** (town hall) contains the flag that de Lugo planted when he arrived from Spain. (The nearby tourist office offers a free plan as well as one-hour walking tours of the old town). To the right, the **Palacio de Nava** is a Baroque mansion that belonged to the Marquis de Villanueva del Prado in the early eighteenth century, when his glittering salon attracted the thinkers of the day. He was also responsible for establishing the Botanic Garden in La Orotava. In between is the massive **Iglesia-Convento de Santa Catalina de Siena**, with a 'Canarian' balcony on the corner from where the nuns can glimpse the outside world.

NOTES

A clean and efficient *tranvía* (tram) service linking La Laguna with Santa Cruz offers splendid views. See http://metrotenerife.com for timetables and prices.

Calle Obispo Rey Redondo traces the blank wall of the convent, past three seventeenth-century mansions that make this the most impressive corner of town. The tourist office is housed in the Casa de Alvarado Bracamonte. Wander down the street to the **Catedral**, where de Lugo is buried behind the altar, and the **Iglesia de la Concepción**, which dates from 1502. Its font was used to baptise converted Guanche leaders. On Calle San Agustin, at No 22, it is possible to see the interior of a mansion, Casa Lercaro, home to a branch of **Museo de Historia y Antropología de Tenerife** (www.museosdetenerife.org; charge). This fine building, with its own small chapel, was built by the Genoan Lercaro family of bankers in 1593; the owner's first son, Francisco, becoming the Lt-Governor of Tenerife. Nearby, at San Agustin 18, the beautifully restored historic *casona* (house) shelters the **Fundación Crisitino de Vera** (www.fundacioncristinodevera.org; free), featuring a collection of paintings by the contemporary Canarian artist Cristino de Vera Reyes.

From the Plaza del Adelantado, Calle Nava y Grimón wends past the peach-coloured walls of the **Convento de Santa Clara** (www.clarisaslalaguna.com), the town's other immense convent housing the Sacred Art Museum (free but donations welcome), which tells its history and displays valuable works including eighteenth- and nineteenth-century paintings, to the Convent of San Miguel de las Victorias Franciscanes. Here, the **Santuario del Santísimo Cristo de La Laguna** contains a figure of Christ commissioned by De Lugo from a Flemish sculptor in 1520. Dripping with 'New World' silver and gold, it is the town's most venerated figure.

Two major museums are within reach of La Laguna. On the outskirts of the town, the **Museo de la Ciencia y el Cosmos** (www.museosdetenerife.org; charge) is a hands-on introduction to cosmology and the planets. The other is yet another branch of the excellent **Museo de Historia y Antropología de Tenerife** in the Casa de Carta in Valle de Guerra (closed for restoration at the time of writing), whose exhibits of popular culture are beautifully laid out, clearly depicting five centuries of rural life on the island.

The fecund Valle de Guerra is a centre for flower growing. Looking down on it is the **Mirador de El Boquerón**, where a map shows the distribution of agriculture; the main crops are bananas, avocados, potatoes, vines and the bird of paradise flower, which has become a symbol of the islands.

A band at a typical romeria fiesta

To the east, beyond the villages of Tegueste and Tejina, **Bajamar** ❺ is a small, old-fashioned resort where people from La Laguna come to soak in the seawater pools. Beyond, **Punto Hidalgo** is a good place for coastal walks, which are signposted from the roundabout at the end of the town. The flower-carpeted *Café Melita* (www.palmelita.es) on the way into Punto Hidalgo has wonderful cakes and pastries, plus views over the sea.

The Anaga Hills

The best view of La Laguna is from the **Mirador Jardín** in the **Monte de las Mercedes**. Gazing over the town and both coasts, it has a helpful explanation of where the lagoon once was and how it gradually faded away. Listen for canaries in the trees and bushes. You might glimpse one, though they are not as brightly coloured in the wild as they are in captivity.

Las Mercedes forest is the start of the **Montañas de Anaga**, a spine of volcanic hills rising to around 1000m (3300ft) with deep valleys running down to the sea, ending in small beaches accessible only by boat or after hours of walking.

The best place to begin is beyond the Jardín at a second *mirador*, **Cruz del Carmen** at 920m (3018ft), though the thickets of heather and fern obstruct the view slightly. The visitor centre for **Parque Rural de Anaga** is here. There is a small exhibition about the natural history of the local area, and an information point with recommended walks.

Just beyond Cruz del Carmen, a turning to the right leads to the **Mirador del Pico del Inglés**, one of the best viewpoints on

View of the city Puerto de la Cruz, Tenerife

WALKING IN THE ANAGA HILLS

Hiking is the best way to explore the Anaga Hills. A starting point is the visitor centre at Cruz del Carmen, or the Albergue Montes de Anaga (http://alberguestenerife.net), where you can obtain maps of the *senderos* (paths). Several walks begin around Las Carboneras, including a route down to the sea at Punto Hidalgo, passing through three identifiable ecosystems. A more dramatic hike is from Chamorga at the end of the road down to Faro de Anaga, the lighthouse on the northeastern tip. Alternatively, book onto a tour with a registered guide such as Anaga Experience (www.anagaexperience.com, charge).

the island. After El Bailadero, beneath which the north–south road tunnels, the road becomes little more than a single track wandering all the way to **Chamorga**, a one-bar community at the end of the road.

The road north of El Bailadero wends through **Taganana**, a community of white houses and palms, which in 1881 felt so cut off it declared itself independent. Its fifteenth-century church is one of the oldest on the island. Beyond, **Playa San Roque** is popular with surfers, who gather on the small beach in front of the buzzy *Bar Playa Casa Africa*. Further on is a string of restaurants at **Roques de las Bodegas**, and at **Benijo** the road dissolves into paths heading over the cliffs.

The dense vegetation of these hills includes the largest natural laurel forest in the Canary Islands, their leaves often dripping with moisture from the misty climate produced by the trade winds. Their prehistoric ecosystem supports bay trees, holly, heather and spurge, while the damp environment keeps alive the ferns, lichen and moss.

There is also a cluster of fascinating cave houses here, such as those at **Chinamada**, where one has been turned into a bar and restaurant called *La Cueva*.

The north coast

Highlights

- **Puerto de la Cruz**, see page 51
- **La Orotava**, see page 55
- **Tacoronte**, see page 57
- **Los Realejos**, see page 59
- **San Juan de la Rambla**, see page 59
- **Icod de los Vinos**, see page 60

The fertile Orotava Valley made the Guanche community here the wealthiest on the island. It did the same for the colonisers who made the most of the ideal growing conditions, building imposing mansions on the proceeds. Villa de la Orotava, as La Orotava was then called, was a gateway up to El Teide. Just below, where the valley arrived at the sea, was Puerto de la Orotava, a handy port from where wine and other products could be shipped abroad.

However, in 1706 a volcanic eruption destroyed the north coast's major port of Garachico. Overnight, Puerto de la Orotava's fortunes burgeoned, and the port was renamed Puerto de la Cruz. When tourism started, this part of the island was where curious visitors ventured, for the climate, the Botanic Gardens, the architecture and for El Teide. By then Alexander Humboldt had paid a visit and made his pronouncements. A *mirador* between La Orotava and Puerto de la Cruz marks the spot where the German naturalist expressed his delight in the view, though he was not so delighted when he returned from his trip up El

NOTES

Plaza Benito Pérez Galdós (also known as La Placeta), named after the Spanish playwright and novelist who was born in Gran Canaria in 1843, is the most pleasant square in La Ranilla. Stop here for a drink or tapas at one of the small restaurants or bars.

Teide to discover his porters had abandoned the plant and mineral samples he had collected, because they thought them unnecessary ballast. It was not long before other botanists and natural philosophers were embarking on the journey up the mountain, followed by the first holidaymakers. When the *Gran Hotel Taoro* (www.granhoteltaoro.com) was built in Puerto de la Cruz in 1890 it was the largest in Spain.

Playa Jardín, Puerto de la Cruz

Puerto de la Cruz

One of the pioneering resorts of Spain, and the oldest in Tenerife, **Puerto de la Cruz** ❻ is a mix of high-rise blocks and, in the centre, handsome old buildings. Gently lit at night, the promenade meanders beneath palm trees and beside black rocks and beaches where foam-tipped waves pound. From the black beaches of Playa Jardín to Playa Martiánez, the seawater pools of Lago Martiánez (www.lagomartianez.es; charge) and the small fishermen's quarter, it is a delight at any time of the day. The lively heart of the town is just inland from the harbour at the **Plaza del Charco de los Camarones**, named after a pool full of shrimp that was once here. There are outdoor cafés, kiosks, bands and the general hum of the town's life.

On the east side of the square, Calle Quintana leads to the sixteenth-century **Ermita de San Juan Batista** and the

Lago Martiánez, designed by Canadian artist César Manrique

eighteenth-century **Iglesia de San Francisco**, effectively one church with the dividing wall removed. The pair shelter a medley of revered paintings of the Madonna.

The street climbs up past two handsome mansions with elegant patios and balconies, now the hotels **Monopol** (www.monopoltf.com) and **Marquesa** (www.hotelmarquesa.com). The *Monopol*, dating from 1742, was the birthplace of Agustín de Bethencourt y Molina, founder of the Madrid Civil Engineers' School and General Director of Ports and Roads for Alexander II of Russia.

The *Marquesa*, more elegant still, has pavement tables perfect for people-watching. The street opens into the Plaza de la Iglesia and the town's principal church, **Iglesia de Nuestra Señora de la Peña de Francia**, built in 1697 with a tower added in 1898. The organ was made in London.

The harbour

The harbour today is small with little activity, and it is hard to imagine it as a stopping point for transatlantic trade. On the eastern side, the distinctive **Casa de la Aduana**, the former customs house and residence of the royal tax collector, shelters Puerto de la Cruz's main **tourist office,** while another part houses an artisanal craft shop. Upstairs the **Museo de Arte Contemporáneo Eduardo Westerdahl, MACEW** (http://artenerife.com/casa-de-la-aduana; free) holds an interesting collection of works by modern Spanish artists and is the town's main cultural centre. To the west, **La Ranilla** is the nicely renovated fishermen's quarter, where you'll find a small **Museo Arqueológico** (free) on Calle El Lomo. It houses a collection of Guanche ceramics. At the far end of La Ranilla, beyond the football ground and municipal swimming pool, the seventeenth-century Castillo San Felipe is a small fort used for exhibitions. It marks the start of the town's main black beach, **Playa Jardín**, which is attractively landscaped behind.

The promenade

On the eastern side of the port, behind the customs house, is the **Plaza de Europa**, a fake castle with genuine cannons, built in 1992 on top of a very handy central car park. The streets behind the square are full of handsome eighteenth- and nineteenth-century mansions with fine doorways and balconies. These give way to the promenade beside the small, rocky San Telmo beach where pools have been cut in the rocks for swimmers. The little white **San Telmo chapel**, dedicated to the patron saint of seamen, was built in 1780 on the site of a coastal battery.

On the point of land beyond here is the enchanting **Lago Martiánez** Ⓐ (https://lagomartianez.es; charge), one of the town's great attractions. With palms, boulders and sky-blue swimming pools, this wonderful area compensates for the lack of decent natural swimming facilities in the town. It was designed by César

Manrique (1919–92), the Lanzarote-born artist who did so much to promote the islands' natural resources. It is easy to spend a whole day in the complex, which has a café and restaurant.

The promenade opens up as it reaches **Playa Martiánez**, the town's other beach that looks towards the cliffs rising to the east.

At the back of the town, the **Jardín Botánico** B (charge), properly known as Jardín de Aclimatación de la Orotava, started life in 1788 as a staging post between the Americas and Europe, allowing tropical and sub-tropical plants to acclimatise to cooler temperatures. The pamphlet that comes with your entry ticket provides a layout of the garden and its species. As a scientific institute, it is especially dedicated to the flora of the Canary Islands, with more

View from Plaza de la Constitución, Orotava, towards the coast

than 30,000 specimens. The **Parque Taoro** ❻ (free), a landscape of gardens and ponds, is also a botanic delight.

La Orotava

La Orotava ❼ is perched high above sea level and its steep streets are studded with the mansions built by the island's wealthy landowners. The church of **San Agustín**, which belonged to a former monastery, has a beautiful wood ceiling and a handsome retable. It sits at one end of the Plaza de la Constitución, which is overlooked by **Liceo de Taoro**, (www.liceodetaoro.es), a grand private club, now open for the public to look around, and the adjacent **Jardínes Marquesado de la Quinta Roja**, also known as Jardín Victoria. These formal gardens were laid out in the nineteenth century around the mausoleum of the Marquis – membership of the Masons precluded him from a burial on consecrated ground. Wilder and more lush are the **Hijuelo del Botánico** gardens just beyond.

Calle Carrera del Escultor Estévez runs along the bottom of Plaza de la Constitución and west past the town's tourist information office. This street then leads past the **Ayuntamiento** (town hall), an imposing Neoclassical edifice that gives a nod to how important La Orotava once was. The square in front of it is brilliantly decorated during Corpus Christi (see page 103) using different coloured earth, flowers, sand and volcanic cinders.

Beyond here, the buildings give a sense of the riches that once flowed through the town. At the top of this road is Tenerife's most famous domestic building, the seventeenth-century **Casa de los Balcones** (www.casa-balcones.com; charge) which, as its name suggests, has superlative wood balconies. For many years it has been associated with the island's lacemaking, along with several other outlets on the island. Staff in traditional costume will show you the best of the wares. Otherwise, you can explore the beautiful patio and, for a small fee, the period rooms upstairs, peopled

Casa de los Balcones

with dummies in costume, including a grandma sound asleep in her bed.

Casa del Turista, the mansion opposite Casa de los Balcones, is almost as grand, and is part of the same outlet for island ware and lace. A few metres further up on the right is the Hospital de la Santísima Trinidad. Inside the courtyard is the revolving drum on the main door via which abandoned babies would be left in the care of the hospital's nuns.

Town church

Below these old streets is the **Iglesia de Nuestra Señora de la Concepción**, La Orotava's main church, built in the sixteenth century and rebuilt after devastating earthquakes in 1705, retaining the original marble altar. Further down the hill, the **Museo de**

Artesanía Iberoamericana (http://artenerife.com; free) displays an intriguing collection of ceramics, baskets, instruments and furniture from all over Latin America.

Opposite, the seventeenth-century **Casa Torrehermosa** sells a selection of crafts, supported by the local government. There are several good restaurants in and around La Orotava, such as *Sabor Canario* and *Victoria* (www.hotelruralvictoria.com), which offer further opportunities to check out the interiors of the town's picturesque mansions.

The wine lands of Tacoronte

East of Puerto de la Cruz, above the motorway on a pleasant rural road, are the villages of **La Mantanza de Acentejo** and **La Victoria de Acentejo**, scenes of the decisive battles between the Guanche *mencey* (chief), Bencomo, and the Spaniard Alonso Fernandez de Lugo. Matanza ('The Slaughter) is where 1200 Spaniards were caught in a trap on 31 May, 1494. Only two hundred escaped, De Lugo among them. He returned with a larger force the following year to win a decisive victory a short distance away at La Vitoria de Acentejo on Christmas Day 1495. Some two thousand Guanche were slaughtered. It is difficult to imagine such scenes of carnage in these quiet hills.

Acres of vineyards mark this region out as **Tacoronte-Acentejo**, the best of the island's five DO wine regions (see page 112). Just beyond La Matanza, the road dips under the motorway to arrive at **Casa del Vino Tenerife** (www.casadelvinotenerife.com), just before entering El Sauzal. This seventeenth-century estate is

NOTES

'Around Orotava is the finest, most fertile land in these islands, and even in the whole of Spain, because on it can be grown and bred anything you may desire.' – Fray Alonso de Espinosa (1594)

an attractive cluster of buildings that includes a wine press and museum (free) with detailed displays in Spanish and English about viniculture on Tenerife. It is an impressive tale, as is the number of different bottles on display – *tinto*, *rosado* and *blanco*. The Casa del Vino has its own bar and restaurant and a room for sampling and buying wine. To further delight the palate, visit the **Tenerife Honey Centre**, also on the La Baranda estate and run by the island council as a centre for extracting and bottling honey.

High above the rocky coast, best seen from La Garañona *mirador*, and set on a slope is **El Sauzal** ❽, where the square outside the town hall teeters down attractive steps beside a waterfall. **Tacoronte**, too, is poised high above the sea and has a cluster of *bodegas* and restaurants. Its historic main square, Plaza del Cristo, is overlooked by a seventeenth-century church and convent of the same name; during Corpus Christi, coloured earth and flowers carpet the square.

Casa del Vino, El Sauzal

Ten minutes' walk down a steep hill, the church of **Santa Catalina** is fronted by a typical balcony. It has two of the finest retables on the island and among its paintings is a fine *Inmaculada* by José Luján Pérez.

The coast at Tacoronte looks tantalisingly close, but the journey down is steep and winding. **Mesa Mar** has a small beach and bars. Just

San Pedro church, El Sauzal

beyond, along a pleasant coast road, **El Pris** is a small bay peppered with fish restaurants.

West of Puerto de la Cruz

The motorway west of Puerto de la Cruz peters out at **Los Realejos**, which it divides between the older, upper part, Realejo Alto, and the lower, modern town, Realejo Bajo. This is the last chapter in the subjugation of the Guanches, where De Lugo pitched camp in 1498 and accepted their surrender and lands. The much-renovated church of Santiago Apóstol in the upper town still has the font where the converted Guanches were baptised.

Beyond Los Realejos, **San Juan de la Rambla** is an attractive, small white village by the sea. Inland, high above, is La Guancha, a quiet artisanal village with fine views.

Icod de los Vinos ⓽ is on the tourist map for its dragon tree, **El Drago Milenario**. Reaching 16m (56ft) with a 20m (20ft) circumference at its base, it is the largest and most ancient on the island. It looms above the main road on the west side of the town, helped in its old age by metal and concrete supports. It's often claimed to be a thousand years old but it's probably more like eight hundred. Near the small park in which the tree stands, is **Mariposario del Drago** (www.mariposario.com; charge), a tropical garden full of butterflies from around the world.

The old town of Icod is one of the most attractive on the island. Its typical buildings are best around the Plaza de Constitución, shaded by palms, oleander and jacaranda, and in Plaza de la Pila, where the nineteenth-century Casa de los Cáceres has been repurposed as an exhibition centre. Icod has long been the centre of a wine-producing area, and you can buy local bottles at the **Museo de Malvasía** (https://museomalvasia.com) in Plaza de la Pila. A wine festival takes place every year on the eve of St Andrew's Day (29 November), when locals ride on sleds down the steep streets of the town making as much noise as possible, in remembrance of the wine barrels once taken down to the port for export.

The dragon tree at Icod de los Vinos

In a little square below the plaza, the church of San

THE DRAGON TREE

The dragon tree (*draecana draco*), which dates from the prehistoric Tertiary period, is unique to the Canary Islands. It held a mystical quality for the Guanches, who saw it as a symbol of fertility and wisdom, using its bark on their shields when they went to war. Its resin, known as dragons' blood, turns red on contact with the air, and was used to embalm the Guanche dead. In Europe other uses were found for it, to dye hair golden, to stain marble red and to varnish violins.

Marcos contains a sacristy and small museum. Among its treasures is a filigree cross made of Mexican silver weighing 47kg (104lb). A much newer attraction in Icod is caving through volcanic lava tubes. The **Cueva del Viento** ⓾ (www.cuevadelviento.net; charge) has over 17km (11 miles) of lava tubes; guided tours depart from the visitor centre.

Pinewoods behind the town stretch up towards El Teide. On the coast **Playa San Marcos** has an attractive small black beach with fishing boats and restaurants.

El Teide

Highlights

- **Las Cañadas del Teide Crater**, see page 63
- **Aguamansa**, see page 65
- **Observatorio Astronómico del Teide**, see page 66
- **Los Roques de García and Los Azulejos**, see page 68
- **Vilaflor**, see page 68
- **Chio**, see page 69

The traditional path up to El Teide for early visitors to the island was from La Orotava. They would be taken by guides with mules up the track used by pumice miners and by the *neveros*, who brought compacted snow down from the tops of the mountains with which they could make ice cream.

Today, four main roads lead up to the **Parque Nacional del Teide** ⓫, so it is accessible from all corners of the island. Unless you are up for a five-hour climb, the last part of the journey is by *teleférico* (cable car), 1.6km (1 mile) north of the *Parador de Cañadas del Teide* hotel and 8km (5 miles) south of the visitor centre. It does not operate during windy weather. You should arrive early in the morning to avoid queues or buy your tickets on the website (www.volcanoteide.com; charge). The highest mountain in Spain is 3718m (12,198ft) above sea level – and it is cold. Snow caps the peak for most of the year and temperatures can dip well below freezing. Yet it is still

El Teide, Spain's highest mountain

surprising to learn how many of the 2.5 million annual park visitors turn up in beachwear.

Most people who alight from the cable car do not want to stroll far, and those who are pregnant or suffer from coronary or respiratory problems should not attempt to do so, as there is fifty percent less oxygen in the air than at sea level. It is possible to walk just beneath the crater. It is also possible to walk on its rim, but to prevent erosion from hikers' boots, the authorities have introduced a system whereby you have to have written permission to do this. Permits can be obtained free from the Parque Nacional del Teide (www.reservasparquesnacionales.es). Apply a couple of months in advance – you will need to take your passport and show your summit permit on the mountaintop.

NOTES

Since the 1966 movie *One Million Years BC*, starring Raquel Welch, El Teide's bleak lands have starred in a number of films and TV series including the 2016 *Jason Bourne* film, the 2010 blockbuster *Clash of the Titans*, and season two of *The Lord of the Rings: The Rings of Power* (2022).

Las Cañadas del Teide Crater

El Teide rises from a great hollow in the centre of the island, a caldera (a crater formed when the cone explodes) that is the remnants of an earlier, much larger volcano, of around 4800m (16,000ft). This flat, pale expanse between the remains of the former crater wall and the peak of El Teide forms the park. In fact, there were two earlier volcanoes, creating two calderas, separated by the mauve and pink barrier of Los Roques de García. Together they form an egg-shaped area 15km (9 miles) across. Lava and ashes have spilled from the volcanoes in a series of eruptions at different times, which explains why the rocks are so varied in texture and colour. Some cooled quickly into jagged formations, others more slowly into smoother, more liquid shapes.

CLIMBING EL TEIDE PEAK

The path to the summit starts approximately 2km (1 mile) east of the *teleférico* (cable car) base, where there is parking space for about a dozen cars and a map of the route. It is a straight walk up, with no scrambling or climbing, and it takes about five hours, during which you will climb around 1400m (4600ft). You can return via the *teleférico*. A fleece and waterproof jacket are recommended, and in winter you should also wear snow glasses. Camping is not allowed in the park, but there is a shelter, the *Refugio de Altavista*, at 3250m (10,650ft). Just beyond the refuge is a nineteenth-century ice cave, where early visitors cooled themselves after the horse ride up from La Orotava.

As the path reaches the top of the *teleférico*, you will need to present your permit (see page 63) and passport to a ranger before continuing along the Telesforo Bravo path to the rim of the crater, through fumaroles emitting sulphurous clouds. The view is absolutely spectacular, and on a clear day you should be able to see all of the Canary Islands.

El Teide lies to the north of the park, and volcanic activity continues around the parasitic cones that sprouted around it. The most recent eruptions have formed a caldera on the summit of El Teide where fumaroles – escape hatches for steam – still blow. In 1798 an explosion created Las Narices del Teide ('Teide's Nostrils') on the south flank. The most recent eruption in the park occurred in 1909 from Montaña Chinyero, which is located in the west. El Teide is considered by experts to be still active.

A number of other peaks rise from the solidified lava in the park. Pico Viejo (3134m/10,282ft), to the southwest of El Teide, was formed a little earlier. The highest point on Las Cañadas del Teide's crater rim is Mt Guajara (2717m/ 8914ft) on the south side of the *Parador de Cañadas del Teide*, and beyond it is the Paisaje Lunar, a haunting lunar landscape. To the north are the large caves of Cueva del Hielo or Cueva de los Cazadores. Around Guajara Pass, which once linked the Orotava road with Vilaflor, are former Guanche huts and many of the island's mummies have been found in caves nearby.

The routes into the park

Once fertile lands scattered with small lakes, the calderas were the summer pastures for the Guanches' sheep and goats. They entered the region through *cañadas*, breaches in the rim of the calderas that give the park its name. These are most visible on the southern side where the Llano de Ucanca is the site of a former lake. The four modern roads into the park rise steeply and there are few other places on earth where the landscape changes so quickly, from lush valleys to the rocky, volcanic terrain of the higher elevations, passing through a cloud level between 1000m and 1500m (3300ft and 5000ft).

Hiking in the volcanic Parque Nacional del Teide

From the north

The road from La Orotava twists and climbs steeply through the moist Orotava Valley, past thatched barns and patches of agricultural land towards the village of **Aguamansa**. Here, there are forest trails through the pines. The village is situated in the cloud level, so if you plan to strike out on a walk, be prepared for some precipitation. Nearby, **Los Organos** is a rock formation that looks like organ pipes. Beyond Aguamansa look for another geological curiosity on the left-hand side of the road, the **Marguerita de Piedra**, a lump of basalt rock that seems to have exploded, forming daisy-like petals. Finally, at 2020m (6630ft), the road is joined by the road from La Laguna and it enters the park at the Portillo Pass.

From the east

The road from La Laguna is also the best route from Santa Cruz, so it can be busy at weekends. Built in the 1940s by the military, this thoroughfare is the straightest, least steep of the four, running along the ridge of the Cumbre Dorsal and providing spectacular views over both coasts. It passes through **La Esperanza**, a place known for its roadside meat restaurants. From here the **Bosque la Esperanza**, a forest of pines and picnic spots, spreads beside the road for a dozen kilometres. On the left, before the first viewpoint at **Mirador de las Flores**, is **Las Raíces**, the spot where Franco and a hundred co-conspirators met at an outdoor lunch in June 1939 to seal their agreements shortly before their attack on the mainland. A monument marks the spot.

At 2400m (7900ft) the road reaches two sky-watching institutions, the **Observatorio Atmosférico de Izaña** (http://izana.aemet.es) and the **Observatorio Astronómico del Teide** (www.iac.es; charge). Teide National Park is designated as a Starlight Reserve, meaning the skies are protected and it's considered one of the best places on earth to stargaze. You can easily see the stars yourself if you head up above the cloud level at sundown or, alternatively, book onto a tour with a local company such as Canary Nature Guide (www.canariasnatureguides.com). If you do, remember to pack layers of warm clothing as the temperature drops dramatically.

The starting point

As the peak looms dramatically into view, the road from La Laguna meets the one from La Orotava at **El Portillo** just before the **visitor**

centre. Moroccan cedars have been replanted here as part of an attempt to rewild deforested areas. Measures to conserve the nature of the park have meant that many paths are closed to vehicles and hikers. Essential maps and guides should be on sale here, but don't count on them being in stock: if you are walking, it is best to try to find decent maps before reaching the park. Videos and displays offer a good grounding in the history of the park and an idea of what to expect. Some tours and guides are advertised or may be available. You can also check out the flora here: Teide daisies flower in the winter snow, pink broom blossoms in May, and the Teide violet a little later. The rock's colour depends on the time of day and the light: the lava is in extraordinary hues of yellows, reds and browns, and there's the shiny black obsidian with which the Guanche made blades for their tools and weapons.

The cable car to the Parque Nacional del Teide

Cable car and Parador de Cañadas del Teide

From the visitor centre it is about 12km (7 miles) to the **teleférico** or cable car. It takes eight minutes and stops 170m (560ft) short of the summit. Refreshments are available at the bottom only. Paths from the top lead to two *miradors* at the foot of the final ascent, for which you need a permit (see page 63). From the viewpoints you can see the jagged rocky and rope-like formations from the mountain's latest lava flows.

The **Parador Las Cañadas del Teide** is the only hotel in the park and it makes an excellent base for an early-morning walk to the summit. The night sky is sparkling, and groups of visitors come to the parador for dinner and astronomy talks.

Nearby, **Los Roques de García** ⓬ are extraordinary gnarled formations that are all that remain from the dividing wall between the two former volcanoes that make up the caldera. Stones near these rocks are deep green from copper oxide, and are known as **Los Azulejos**, the glazed tiles.

From the southwest

From Playa de las Américas, Los Cristianos and the other resorts of the southwest, the ninety-minute drive up to the park starts either at Arona or at Granadilla de Abona, and climbs steeply to where the roads converge at **Vilaflor** ⓭. Situated at an altitude of 1400m (4600ft), this village claims to be the highest in Spain, and its population of 1800 makes it the island's smallest municipality. It stands among volcanic cones in the middle of pine woods, of which the Pino Gordo, the fat pine, is the finest example, 65m (215ft) tall and 10m (30ft) in circumference. Vilaflor is a good base for exploring the mountains and is the nearest village to the park, where there are no shops or commercial outlets. Its sixteenth-century church was founded by a Catalan colonialist, Pedro Soler, who first put this land to work for the Spanish. Vilaflor is a popular stopping point, so if you wish to stay overnight, try to book a hotel in advance.

It is noticeably cooler here than on the coast and it snows in winter. Generally, however, when the weather is poor on the coast, it is sunny up above the clouds. The bare earth on the tidy, geometrical terraces is covered with lava pebbles called *picón*, which help to retain the moisture. There is no shortage of water, and underground springs provide the island with bottled water. There is also enough moisture for a healthy agricultural industry of tomatoes, potatoes and grapes. These must be among the highest vineyards in the world.

Just outside Vilaflor is the **Ermita San Roque** with a *mirador*. This is followed by two more roadside *miradors*: **Mirador de las Pinos** and, just beyond a large bottling plant, **Mirador las Lajas**. Both make pleasant picnic stops.

From the west

The road from the west coast wiggles from the white village of **Chio** at 680m (2240ft), from where there is a panoramic view back over the coast around the high cliffs of Los Gigantes. Less twisting than the route through Vilaflor, it climbs through the inhospitable,

View from the top of El Teide

jagged clinker and dark grey lava to reach the thoroughfare from Vilaflor at **Boca de Tauce**. Here a breach in the caldera rim lets the road through into the lunar landscape of the park.

The northwest

Highlights

- **Garachico**, see page 71
- **Masca**, see page 75
- **El Tanque**, see page 76
- **Los Gigantes**, see page 77
- **San Juan**, see page 78

Castillo de San Miguel, Garachico

The northwest of the island is one of its richest and most diverse pockets. Deeply rural, it has many hidden corners as well as popular spots, none of which are ever very crowded. Much of the area is covered by **El Teno Rural Park** ⓮, a conservation area of more than 80sq km (30sq miles) based on the Teno massif, one of the geologically oldest parts of Tenerife. There is a range of vegetation between the hills and valleys, and wildflowers are in abundance. Birdlife is also plentiful, both in the hills and around the northern coastal plain, and seabirds can be seen from Punto El Teno. **Isla Baja** is the name given to the region that covers the districts of Buenavista, Garachico, Los Silos and El Tanque. Its capital, Garachico, makes a good base.

A string of traditional houses and *fincas* (country estates) throughout the region have been converted into places to stay.

Old architecture in Garachico

Garachico

An hour before dawn on 5 May 1706, the sky above **Garachico** ⓯ was illuminated by the eruption of El Volcán Negro, 8km (5 miles) inland. It was not long before two streams of lava were scorching their way through forests and vineyards towards the coast. Alarmed, the people of Garachico, Tenerife's main port, watched it coming. Genoese merchants abandoned their mansions and monks and nuns left their religious houses, fleeing the path of the boiling lava. In the harbour, ships trading in sugar and wine could only put to sea and watch as the river of molten earth barged and burned its way through the town's buildings and filled up the harbour, turning the sea into a boiling cauldron. Garachico's days of glory were over – it would never be the same again.

If you venture to the **Mirador de Garachico** you can look down on the white buildings that cover the curve of lava jutting out into the sea and make out the paths of the two devastating rivers of molten rock.

Santa Ana in Garachico

Garachico today is a handsome town of almost five thousand that is so unhurried that it needs no traffic lights. Its seafront is given over to leisure, with a municipal pool, a football pitch and a modern marina. Once or twice a year the sea comes in and batters the pitch, though most days the blue water looks benign, especially where it laps the black swimming rocks around the **Castillo de San Miguel**. With its bar and restaurant, this is a good place to look out across the sea as the sun sets. The castle, dating from 1570, has a collection of shells from around the world, and provides a viewing point from its battlements.

Just inland from the castle is the pretty **Plaza de Juan Gonzales de la Torre**, at the back of which the former land gate to the harbour has been excavated. There is a huge seventeenth-century wine press here, too, a reminder of the time when locally produced Malvasía wine made Garachico – and Tenerife – rich. Nearby, a monument is dedicated to Cristóbal de Ponte, the Genoan banker who founded the town. A few steps from the square is the parish church of **Santa Ana**. Rebuilt after the eruption, it contains a magnificent crucifix by Martin de Andujar, a Sevillian craftsman, and a figure of Christ made by the Indigenous Purepecha (Tarasco) in Mexico. Beside the church, the small, curved Calle Esteban de Ponte traces the seafront. The De Ponte family house is located here, alongside other impressive seventeenth-century buildings opposite the tourist information office.

The main square, Plaza de la Libertad, which remains much as it must have looked before the eruption, is shaded and has several restaurants. A statue of the Venezuelan revolutionary leader, Simón Bolívar, has been added because his mother, María Concepción Palacio y Blanco, was born in the town. It was the first sculpture of the great liberator to be erected in Spain. On the southern side of the square is the palace of the counts of Gomera.

Dominating the eastern side is the church of **Nuestra Señora de los Angeles** and the eighteenth-century former **Convento de San Francisco**. The latter has a pair of fine courtyards and is home to the **Casa de la Cultura**, a cultural centre hosting exhibitions, a library and a small natural history museum. On the northern side, the ochre walls wrap around *La Quinta Roja*, a beautiful hotel with a bar and restaurant.

It is also a hub of activity in the region, with information on walks and tours. Drop in to find out what is going on – and look out for the turtles in the garden.

Another smart hotel is the *San Roque*, in the Casa Noriega just to the west of the square, and its contemporary sculptures show the town's fondness for the arts as well as its heritage.

Monument to the Emigrants

West of Garachico

The road heading west out of Garachico trails past the **Playa del Muelle** and climbs up to a headland where the **Monumento a los Emigrantes Canarios** shows a figure with a suitcase and a hole in his heart setting off in search of a better life in America. There has been large-scale emigration from this corner of the island, especially to Venezuela, and many towns and villages celebrate the day of Nuestra Señora de Buen Viaje, Our Lady of the Good Journey, on 31 August.

The nearest decent beach to Garachico is a little further on, the **Playa La Caleta de Interián**.

As the road swerves west, the countryside starts to flatten, smoothing a path first through sleepy **Los Silos** and arriving at **Buenavista del Norte**. Built around a central square with a small pavilion, its low, white houses have a languid, southern feel. The church of Nuestra Señora de los Remedios was refurbished after a serious fire in 1966.

The hamlet of Masca

The road from Buenavista continues all the way to **Faro de Teno** ⓰, the lighthouse at the island's northwestern tip, which attracts birdwatchers on the lookout for ospreys, Barbary falcons and Cory's shearwaters. Road signs warn motorists of the dangers of landslides, which tend to occur mainly in windy and wet weather. La Gomera and La Palma creep in view as you reach the headland, and at the lighthouse at **Punto del Teno** you can see down the entire west coast.

From Buenavista the road sweeps inland, past vines and signs for cheese for sale, and up through an ever-changing tangle of vegetation, with poppies lining the road. Among geological curiosities is the **Montañeta del Palmar**, which has been sliced like a cake for the extraction of *picón*, a gravel made of lava which is spread on agricultural land to retain moisture in the soil.

At the **Mirador del Baracán** there is a view down over both coasts. Bees hum as they potter about the aromatic plants, swifts dart overhead, and walking paths wiggle away into Teno Park.

Masca

The jewel of Tenerife's northwest is **Masca** ⓱, a cluster of buildings tipped over the side of the hill in a stunning setting above the sea. Approached over the hills from Buenavista or along the dramatic ribbon of road that flutters down from Santiago del Teide, Masca is not much more than a hamlet. It has approximately a hundred inhabitants and it was off the tourist map until the road to it was eventually constructed in 1972.

Near the roadside, where cars squeeze into the few parking spaces, there are a couple of restaurants with terraces where you can eat cactus ice cream with goat's yoghurt and honey, or sip on cactus and papaya juice. Among the clutch of attractive buildings just below is a small museum of local finds.

The forest fires of July 2007, which burnt more than 15,000 hectares (37,000 acres) of land, engulfed the town and destroyed half the buildings. Fortunately, no lives were lost as the village was evacuated in time. Located in a traditional house, a small **Museo Etnográfico** offers a glimpse into the life of the town's former inhabitants. One of the main draws is the six-hour round hike into the narrow **Barranco de Masca** and down to the beach. Due to Masca's soaring popularity over recent years, there are now restrictions in place if you want to hike the ravine, which includes buying a ticket (www.caminobarrancodemasca.com; charge), the proceeds of which are funnelled into conservation efforts. Tickets include transport from Santiago del Teide, but you have to book boat tickets from the bottom of the ravine back to town separately if you are planning to only walk one way.

El Tanque

The road above the coast at Garachico leads to **El Tanque**, a district of five hamlets scattered among pastureland in patchworks of fields between sweeping mountains. The main village of El Tanque overlooks the sea and centres on a corn exchange, the Casa de la Alhóndiga, that was once the town's meeting place. Mirador Lomo Molino is yet another great viewpoint on this route.

Church in Santiago del Teide

The road now climbs to reach the **Erjos** mountain pass (1117m/3664ft), where paths wend down to old farmhouses tucked into the folds of the valleys. This pass divides north from south, and from here the full southern heat brings only cacti and *malpaís* to the dry scrubland. It meets the road from Masca at **Santiago del Teide**, a sunny white town cradled in a broad valley. To the east looms **Montaña del Chinyero**, the last volcano to erupt on the island, in 1909.

The village of **Arguayo**, situated just beyond, is famous for its ceramics, and includes the **Centro Alfarero y Museo Etnográfico Cha Domitila** (www.artenerife.com/centros-alfareros; free), a museum and workshop showcasing traditional handmade earthenware.

NOTES

People from Tenerife are colloquially known as *chicharerros*. This is rooted in the word *chicharo* – the mackerel fish that is common in the waters swirling around the island. When the rich people of then-capital La Laguna spoke down their noses about the impoverished mackerel fisherfolk of Santa Cruz (then a fishing town and port), they referred to them as *chicharerros*. But the *chicharerros* had the last laugh when the capital city status was transferred to Santa Cruz de Tenerife in 1833.

Los Gigantes to San Juan

Boats that sail to Masca bay are just part of the flotilla of pleasure craft berthed in **Los Gigantes** ⓲. This port, at the foot of a steep hill, is the island's premier diving centre (see page 96) and the possibilities for watersports are endless. The port looks directly out at the *acantilado*, the foreboding sheer cliff that dominates the skyline – this is the dramatic 800m (2625ft) wall of the Teno massif, where the boat-less Guanche thought that the world came to an abrupt end. Looking out at it today, it's easy to imagine how they came to such a conclusion. The cliff also plunges fairly rapidly beneath the sea – perfect for deep-diving enthusiasts.

Los Gigantes has a tiny black-sand beach, but there is a good swimming pool, Piscina la Laguillo, just up from the port, and a much larger beach, **Playa de Arena**, at sister resort **Puerto Santiago**, which is within easy striking distance. You might also take a dip at Oasis pool, which has a short slide, splendid views of the cliffs and a restaurant. The next resort of **Alcalá**, also based

Los Gigantes harbour

on a fishing port, has natural pools to swim in. **San Juan**, about 8km (5 miles) south of Los Gigantes, manages to retain its character as a working fishing port, despite the new development. Around the bay, a sand beach has been created. On Wednesday and Sunday mornings a food and craft market attracts visitors from across the region. There are also a couple of snorkelling and scuba-diving schools offering the chance to see rays, cuttlefish and octopus.

Inland from San Juan, **Guía de Isora** is a rural community where potatoes and tomatoes grow. Its church has two Madonnas by José Luján Pérez.

The south

Highlights

- **Playa de las Américas**, see page 80
- **Los Cristianos**, see page 82
- **Adeje**, see page 83
- **Las Galletas**, see page 84
- **Los Abrigos**, see page 84
- **Granadilla de Abona**, see page 86
- **Ancient temples**, see page 87
- **Candelaria**, see page 88

Served by Reina Sofia airport, the south of the island is where it is hot, so this is where holidaymakers flock, mainly to the resorts in the *municipios* of Adeje and Arona, in the merged touristopolis of Playa de las Américas and Los Cristianos. Hotels, apartments and villas continue to mushroom along the coast, bringing greenery to the *malpaís*, the badlands. Near the airport is Tenerife's longest beach, El Médano. The shoreline back towards Santa Cruz is studded with rocky bays and small fishing ports such as Los Abrigos and Abona. An upper road, from Granadilla de Abona to Güímar – where Thor Heyerdahl discovered mystic 'pyramids' – passes through a string of small villages with views all down the coast. Some 15km (10 miles) before Santa Cruz the road drops to the

Sunlounging in the south

coast around Candelaria, the most important pilgrimage town in the Canary Islands, and home to the giant Menceyes sculptures by Tinerfeño artist José Abad.

The big resorts

You have to know where you are going when you arrive in **Playa de las Américas** ⓳. Built out of nothing in the 1970s, it has no natural centre, the roads are often not signposted, and directions are generally given in terms of hotel names. Most of the seafront belongs to the four- and five-star hotels, and often the closest you will get to the beach in a vehicle is their car parks.

The sheer range of waterfront accommodation is spectacular, from Canarian villages to Mexican *haciendas*, courtesans' boudoirs and the glories of ancient Rome. Most ambitious is **Mare Nostrum** (https://marenostrumresort.com), a 'resort' of five-star hotels that look like something out of a Cecile B. de Mille epic. It includes the *Mediterranean Palace*, the *Cleopatra Palace and Sir Anthony* hotels – all three offering pools, bars and restaurants. The large **Playa de las Vistas** lies between here and Los Cristianos, but the main beaches of **Playas de Troya** and **Playa del Bobo** are to the north of the **Barranco del Rey**.

Playa de las Américas

LA GOMERA

Christopher Columbus's last port of call before he headed into the unknown in 1492 was the island of La Gomera, now just thirty minutes away from Los Cristianos on Fred Olsen's Australian-built *Benchijigua*. When you step ashore at San Sebastián you will find yourself in quite a different world. This quiet, underpopulated speck is just 24km (15 miles) across, but you need to venture away from the port to discover its rural secrets. At its centre is the Parque Nacional de Garajonay, a UNESCO World Heritage Site, which you pass through to reach the lovely Valle de Gran Rey. For the sunniest beach, take a bus to Playa de Santiago. One of the world's toughest sporting events, the Atlantic Challenge (www.worldstoughestrow.com) kicks off from San Sebastián every December, when rowers teams in 7.3m (24ft) boats test their mettle on the 5000km (3000 mile) journey across the Atlantic to Antigua.

There is a tourist information point at this gully, which is near the rowdy **Veronicas** strip, a hub of more than a hundred nightclubs. Technically the *barranco* marks the municipal boundary between Arona and Adeje. The coast north of here is the more upmarket **Costa Adeje**, which drifts seamlessly into the giant hotels of San Eugenio, Torviscas, Fañabe, Playa del Duque, Playa Paraiso and Calle Salvaje. The small harbour of **Puerto Colón** in San Eugenio is the centre for water activities, dolphin- and whale-watching boats, and diving (see page 96). Inland from the port, the large **Aqualand** water park (www.aqualand.es; charge) is just one of myriad activities.

There are no limits to entertainment possibilities in and around Playa de las Américas (see page 101). On Thursdays and Saturdays follow the crowds to the market held near Plaza del Duque at the north of the resort.

The plaza itself is home to a shopping centre, with upmarket boutiques as well as all the usual chain stores.

LORO PARQUE AND SIAM PARK

Siam Park on the Costa Adeje might be a tourist big-hitter, but it is mired in controversy as the sibling of Loro Parque in Puerto de la Cruz, a marine park that profits from degrading orca and dolphin shows with no educational or conservational value. Three orcas died prematurely at Loro Parque between 2021 and 2022: 2-year-old Ula, 20-year-old Kohana and 17-year-old Skyla – decades shorter than the natural life expectancy of 30 to 50 years. Skyla was just 2 years old when she was ripped away from her mother Kalina, shipped thousands of miles to Tenerife and caged for fifteen years without ever experiencing freedom. Skyla's father, Tilikum, captured the world's attention in 2013 documentary *Blackfish*, which detailed his suffering at SeaWorld, revealing how the frustration of confinement led him to kill three people, including trainer Dawn Brancheau. In the wild, many orcas and dolphins stay with their families for life and can swim up to 225km (140 miles) every day (dolphins up to 100km/60 miles). However, those in captivity are often in cramped concrete tanks away from their family, compromising their physical and mental health. Nonetheless, Loro Parque continues to breed captive orcas. We recommend readers do not visit Loro Parque or Siam Park. Instead embark on whale-watching or dolphin-spotting trips to view these majestic creatures in the wild; Biosean (www.biosean.com) and Blue Jack Sail (www.bluejacksail.com) are among the ethical tour operators.

La Caleta just to the north of Playa del Duque is home to some of the island's most exclusive hotels, but the waterfront is still an enticing spot for its seafood restaurants.

Los Cristianos

The starting point of these resorts was the port of **Los Cristianos** ⓴, which lies on the south side of Playa de las Américas. They are separated by the volcanic cone of Montaña Chayofita, but it is otherwise hard to see the join, and you can walk from one to the other along a 7km (4-mile), palm-lined promenade, dotted with pizzerias and souvenir shops. The port is still active, its ferries serving the neighbouring islands of El Hierro, La Palma and La Gomera. The south-facing **Playa los Cristianos** and **Playa de las Vistas** are sheltered, and the sea is shallow and safe. Puerto Colón is the main departure point for whale and dolphin-watching trips (see page 96).

Los Cristianos has an authentic atmosphere around its main pedestrian street, Avenida de Suecia, where there are inexpensive *pensións*, and above the Paseo Marítimo, where a row of restaurants and bars offer sea views. Events and exhibitions are staged in the **Centro Cultural**, which is home to the tourist office. At the far end of the beach an open area is the site of a lively Sunday market.

The municipal towns

Inland are the municipality's main towns, Adeje and Arona. **Adeje**, the former seat of the Guanche government, has never minded much how it made money. At the top of the town are the remains of the **Casa Fuerte**, the stronghold of Pedro, Count of Gomera and one of the Genoese de Ponte family, who ruled the roost along this coast. He fell in with another rogue, the Elizabethan pirate John Hawkins, and together they conducted illegal trade with South America, as well as dealing in enslaved Africans. Hawkins, who was later

San Sebastian de la Gomera's promenade

knighted for his role in defeating the Spanish Armada, was the first Englishman to become involved in the slave trade, in 1562. The town has a pleasant, if steep Rambla, lined with bars and cafés, that leads to the Iglesia Santa Ursula, with a Gobelins tapestry among its contents and an eighteenth-century chapel that was once part of a Franciscan convent.

Turn left at the top of the Rambla for the Casa Fuerte, and then up to *Otelo* (www.otelorestaurante.com), the restaurant at the entry point to the **Barranco del Infierno** (www.barrancodelinfierno.es; charge), one of the most dramatic ravines on the island and the main calling card for many visitors. Good walking shoes and at least a litre of water per person are needed for the round-trip walk up to the waterfall at the head of the *barranco*, which takes around three hours. There is a surprising amount of plant life along the way. If nothing else, this hike can give those staying at the main resorts a flavour of the island's true nature.

Along the south coast

New developments ripple around the southern tip of the island, at **Palm-Mar** and the **Costa del Silencio**, which are entirely purpose-built communities. Between the two, **Las Galletas** is a little fishing port swamped by hotels and apartments, but where fish is still sold on the quayside every morning, bringing many *tinerfeños* in search of a good catch. The seafront is a pleasant stroll, with a cluster of restaurants and cafés serving fresh fish and tapas.

Perhaps the best place for seafood is **Los Abrigos**, the next port along, where restaurants line the lane leading down to the port.

The longest beach in Tenerife stretches several kilometres around the **Montaña Roja**, a volcanic lump that punctuates the bleak acres of arid coast by the airport. Cars line the road but there are few amenities on the khaki-coloured sand, which stretches from the naturist beach of **La Tejita** to the small port of **El Médano** ㉑. Many visitors come here in search of swell, for this is the haunt of serious windsurfers, and major championships have been held with the aid of the *alisios*, the steady northeast trade winds.

The building that breaks the beachscape is the *Playa Sur Tenerife* (www.hotelplayasur.es), which has been catering to windsurfers for decades. El Médano, at the end of the beach, has accommodation and restaurants.

Further along, **Poris de Abona** is a small community studded with seafood restaurants and a little beach but increasing development.

Granadilla de Abona to Güímar

Just outside El Médano on the road up to Granadilla de Abona is the **Cueva del Hermano Pedro**, the cave where the shepherd boy

Montaña Roja near El Médano, visible from Reina Sofia airport

Peter de Betancurt prayed as a child. Of Norman descent, Brother Peter was born on 19 March 1626, at Vilaflor. At 23 he left for the Americas where he became a missionary in Guatemala and did charitable work among the poor, for which he was canonised in 2002. The cave is now a pilgrim site.

The old town of **Granadilla de Abona** ㉒ can seem deserted after the clamour of the coast. Clock chimes reverberate from the central church, dedicated to St Anthony of Padua. Many of the houses in the old town have been restored, especially in Calle Arquitecto Morrero, just down from the church, where one has become a *casa rural*. Next door, the small **Museo de la Historia de Granadilla de Abona** (free) is a museum of local history.

Parque Etnográfico Pirámides de Güímar

The upper road continues through sleepy old villages surrounded by terraced fields, many of them abandoned. At **Arico el Nuevo** there is also a sense of desertion, of pretty old buildings done up due to being granted historical importance.

The road dives in and out of a succession of deep gullies, the *barrancos*. Pigeons and doves of every colour appreciate the rocks for nesting, while the larger caves have been put to good use as storage space. The **Mirador de Don Martín** frames fine views view the Valle de Güímar where pineapple, avocado, banana, chirimoya, guava, cereal and vines are cultivated.

Ancient temples

Some of the dry-stone terraces here, known as *molleros* or *majones*, look like the bases of pyramids and it is no surprise to find the **Parque Etnográfico Pirámides de Güímar** ㉓ (www.piramidesdeguimar.es; charge) above the town of Güímar. This park is the work of an extraordinary man, Thor Heyerdahl, who lived in Tenerife from 1994 until his death in 2002. In that time, he discovered what he believed to be the Guanches' cult of building flat-topped, step-sided pyramids for sun worship. Shipowner and fellow Norwegian, Fred Olsen, bought land for the park and helped to develop it into a research centre.

Through Heyerdahl's expeditions on the balsa raft *Kon-Tiki* and the reed raft *Ra*, he made connections between the civilisations of Egypt and Mexico. Several acres of buildings have been uncovered. Replicas of his rafts are on show, and the links between the Indigenous peoples of North Africa, the Americas and the Pacific are speculated upon in a museum.

Güímar

Güímar is a working town of 19,000, known for its wines and traditional *tascas* (see page 114). It has two good churches, both with coffered *mudéjar* ceilings. The parish church at the top of the

Guanche chiefs, Candelaria

town has an exceptionally elaborate silver altarpiece, and the curiously arranged church of San Domingo, in the former monastery of the same name, is by the town hall in a shady square.

The tourist office is in the Casa de Artesana on the main shopping street, where you can find information on walks in the Malpaís de Güímar. This semi-desert wasteland surrounds the Montaña Grande below the town and spreads down to **Puertito de Güímar** on the coast. Here there is a pebble beach, and outside the town, in the direction of the *Club Náutico* (www.nauticoguimar.com), you'll find a sandy shore.

Candelaria

The name Candelaria, 'giver of light', means only one thing in the Canary Islands: a venerated Madonna, who is the islands' patron saint. The town of **Candelaria** ㉔, on the coast, is dominated by the 1950s basilica (free) that contains her image, and thousands of pilgrims gather in the square outside every August on the Feast of the Assumption, when the conversion of the Guanches to Christianity is re-enacted.

Lining the sea side of the square are statues by José Abad of the seven Guanche *menceyes*, or chiefs, who were in power at the time of De Lugo's conquest. Six of them didn't have too much to be thankful for when Christianity arrived. One, however, the *mencey* of Güímar, was already halfway to becoming a Christian without realising it. Inside the church the story of the discovery of the Madonna and her healing powers is told in delightful but murky paintings. They show the wooden Madonna holding Jesus in one hand and a candle in the other, arriving on the shore in 1392. Two shepherds discovered her, and one of them cut his hand on his knife while trying to ascertain if the statue was alive.

The wound stopped bleeding the moment he touched her. When news spread, the *mencey* of Güímar, who was the shepherd's leader, had a shrine built for the Madonna, and when the Spanish conquerors arrived, they convinced him that his conversion was underway. De Lugo was thus able to persuade him to join the Spaniards in their subjugation of the island's Guanche communities.

Basílica de Nuestra Señora de la Candelaria

As well as an interesting ceramics workshop and museum, Centro Alfarero de Candelaria (www.artenerife.com/centros-alfareros; free), try to catch the large, bustling craft market in the main square every other Friday. An agricultural market is held every Wednesday and Saturday.

The tourist office has information on the town as well as walks into the surrounding countryside.

Windsurfer picking up the trade winds at El Médano

Things to do

Tenerife's highlights and attractions lie in its natural resources. With a pleasant climate and a diverse landscape of dramatic coasts and exotic interior, the island is ripe for outdoor adventures. The ocean, dropping steeply to the depths of the Atlantic, is a favourite for divers, and there is whale- and dolphin-watching further out at sea. That said, there's more to Tenerife than nature, as the Tenerife calendar is packed with festivals and events, sport competitions and music concerts.

Outdoor activities

Many visitors come to Tenerife to walk in the hills and appreciate the abundant flora and search out unique fauna. Much of the island is given over to parks and nature reserves, making it a hiking and biking paradise. Other popular outdoor activities include horseriding, golf, birdwatching, jeep safaris and quad tours.

Walking and hiking

The island is crisscrossed by tracks and footpaths, including a growing crop of designated walking routes. Tourist offices provide free leaflets on hikes in the Orotava Valley, the Anaga Hills and Teno Rural Park. More ambitious trekkers will want to conquer the lavascapes of the *cañadas* around El Teide, and can find routes at the information centre for the Parque Nacional de las Cañadas del Teide (see page 62). The Mirador Cruz del Carmen visitor hub has details on walking in the Anaga Hills, where the *Albergue Montes de Anaga* (www.alberguestenerife.net) makes a good base.

Other hotels that are good launchpads for walking are *La Quinta Roja* (http://quintaroja.com) in Garachico for the northwest and the *VillAlba Spa Hotel* (www.hotelvillalba.com) in Vilaflor for the southwest. Patea Tus Montes (www.pateatusmontes.com) offers guided hikes around the island, as well as climbing and biking.

Cycling near El Teide

Bikes, karting and ziplining

Mountain bikes can be hired in main tourist centres. Try Cycling in Tenerife (www.cyclingintenerife.com), which organises guided tours for both road and mountain-bike enthusiasts. Bike Point Tenerife (www.bikepointtenerife.com) offers bike rental (including e-bikes) as well as tours for different levels. It is also possible to hire motorbikes, with options ranging from 125cc scooters (€36 a day) to 1200cc models (€99 a day). Check out Motorcycle Hire Tenerife (http://motorcyclehire-tenerife.com).

You can take a spin on a quad bike at Quad Safari (www.quad-tenerife.com), and Quad Excursions Tenerife (https://quadexcursionstenerife.com) provides various tours, including explorations of the coast and forests, as well as trips to Teide or Masca.

Jeep tours are available from Tamarán Alquiler Jeep Safari (www.tamaran.com) in Playa de las Américas. In Santa Cruz, the Forestal Park Tenerife (www.forestalparktenerife.es) is an outdoor adventure playground for intrepid types, offering ziplining and canopy walks high among the treetops.

Flora spotting

The rich flora, which brightens the island throughout the year, is one of Tenerife's main calling cards. May and June, when the roadsides are overwhelmed with flowers, are the best months to visit, but there is something to see all year round. Endemic flora can be found in many different habitats: Cañada del Teide supports alpine plants such as the Teide echium ('Pride of Tenerife'), while desert-like species thrive around El Médano in the *malpaís* lands of the south. Some of these are very rare, and no fewer than nineteen plants have been identified as now being under threat.

When the islands were used as a staging post between the 'New World' and Spain, many South American species were introduced. Some can be seen at the Jardín Botánico in Puerto de la Cruz.

The Museo de la Naturaleza y Arqueología (www.museosdetenerife.org; charge) in Santa Cruz offers a comprehensive account

***Echium wildpretii*, or the 'Tower of Jewels', a native plant to Tenerife**

of the island's flora, and its shop has several books and charts on the subject.

Birdwatching

Tenerife is not abundant with birds, but there are some unusual species that can be spotted, particularly those unique to the island (see page 10). The best places to see seabirds are around the lighthouses on the three extreme points of the island: Faro de Teno, Faro de la Rasca and Faro de Anaga.

Look out for notices about organised local walks. Recommended books include *A Birdwatcher's Guide to the Canary Islands* by Tony Clarke and David Collins; *Finding Birds in the Canary Islands* by Dave Gosney; and *Where to Watch Birds in Tenerife* by Eduardo García del Rey.

Horseriding

Stables offering rides through the countryside include La Caldera del Rey at Costa Adeje, catering for children and adults. You might also try Centro Hípico del Sur (www.centrohipicodelsur.com).

Golf

Tenerife has nine golf courses and several hotels with specialist packages. One of Spain's oldest courses, the 1932-opened Real Club de Golf de Tenerife (www.rcgt.es), is the island's longest established. Found near Los Rodeos airport and graced with excellent views, it looks rather like an English park. The other option in the north is the

NOTES

There are more than forty high spots for paragliders to jump from. Courses and flights are available at Tenerfly (www.tenerfly.com). The Canary Island Air Sports Federation, FECDA, (www.fecda.org) offers detailed information on paragliding routes in Tenerife.

Buenavista (www.buenavistagolf.es), designed by Seve Ballesteros. Courses in the south include Golf Las Américas (www.golflasamericas.com), Golf Costa Adeje (www.golfcostaadeje.com), Golf del Sur (www.golfdelsur.es) and the Amarilla Golf and Country Club (www.amarillagolf.es); the latter two are both in San Miguel de Abona.

Kitesurfing is a popular watersport in Tenerife

Water activities

Just about every water-borne activity it is possible to think of is available on the west and south coasts of the island. Some, like whale-watching trips and scuba diving, allow you to experience the area's unique wildlife, while others, such as windsurfing, take advantage of the superb natural conditions.

Diving

The waters swirling around the island swiftly drop to dramatic depths, concealing caves, caverns and a diversity of ocean life that have made Tenerife one of the most popular diving destinations in the world. Sea temperatures are conducive year-round, from an average 20°C (68°F) in winter to 24°C (75°F) in summer. Tuna, barracuda, sting rays, eagle rays and morays are among the big fish; rainbow wrasse and trigger fish are just a couple of the small delights. Sponges, anemones, and red and yellow

NOTES

Swimming in the sea is relatively safe around the island on the designated beaches, but currents and waves can develop, creating powerful undertows. Look out for a red flag flown, indicating that conditions are unsafe for swimming.

gorgonias also lie in wait. Though the waters plunge to 2000m (6500ft), there is a legal depth of 40m (130ft) imposed on dives, many of which are multilevel. Operators offer equipment rental and courses from beginner to divemaster, as well as video and filmmaking possibilities. Most diving centres operate on the west coast, with companies concentrated in Los Gigantes, such as Los Gigantes Dive Center (www.divingtenerife.co.uk), Playa San Juan, Los Cristianos and around the headland in Las Galletas.

Whale- and dolphin-watching trips

The clear, warm waters between Tenerife and La Gomera are home to pilot whales and bottlenose dolphins, which can be seen all year round. The strait of water was declared Europe's first UNESCO Whale Heritage Area in 2021. Choose operators with sustainable credentials – look out for companies with the 'Barco Azul Blue Boat' stamp of approval, such as Biosean (www.biosean.com) and Blue Jack Sail (www.bluejacksail.com). A glass-bottom catamaran, the *Royal Delfin* (www.tenerifedolphin.com), operates out of Puerto Colón.

Windsurfing

Windsurfers hotfoot it to El Médano, where the bay between the town and the Montaña Roja is one of the world's top ten venues for the sport. The *Playa Sur Tenerife Hotel* hires boards and is one of the main places to hang out. Other good windsurfing spots include the beaches Playa El Cabezo and La Jaquita.

Spectator sports

Football is the top spectator sport, with Club Deportivo Tenerife – the *blanquiazules* (blue and whites) – the main team, playing at the Heliodoro Rodriguez Lopez Stadium in Santa Cruz, generally on Sunday afternoons.

Another, more curious spectator sport is *Lucha Canaria*, a popular event that takes place in village halls and special *terreros* all over Tenerife. It is played on a league basis, in which teams of twelve wrestlers fight individual bouts (*bregas*) in sand rings 10m (33ft) in diameter. The object is to force any part of your opponent's body to the floor using whatever means you can. Exhibition bouts are often staged as part of local fiestas when *juego de palo* or *banot*, a

Tenerife is Europe's first UNESCO Whale Heritage Area

traditional stick-fight, is frequently also held.

NOTES

The Tinerfeño calendar is full of sporting events. At Punta Blanca and during the Tenerife Grand Slam, you can witness the best young surfers ride the swells. If wheels are more your bag than waves, watch as cyclists whizz by as part of the Vuelta al Teide (www.vteide.com) race each May. Trail runners should seek out Tenerife Bluetrail (www.tenerife.utmb.world) in March, where athletes test their mettle on El Teide. Every October, runners also traverse Parque Rural de Anaga for the Santa Cruz Extreme competition (www.santacruzextreme.com).

Culture

Music and dance play a big part in festivities on Tenerife, including the island-wide Baile de Magos in May where you'll hear traditional Canarian folk music, or the Noche en Blanco ('White Night') street concerts each November in La Laguna where local and famous musicians and acts take to the stage after dark. Meanwhile, concert venues across the island welcome international stars and shows all year round, as well as providing space for local talent. The **Auditorio de Tenerife** (www.auditoriodetenerife.com) in Santa Cruz is the home of the admired Orquesta Sinfónica de Tenerife, whose performances run from the beginning of September until the end of July. It is also the main venue for the island's opera and dance. In the south you'll find the Auditorio Infanta Leonor (www.arona.org/auditorio) and **Pirámide de Arona**.

Theatre and performance go hand in hand with the Tenerife way of life – celebrations are always boisterous affairs – and yet surprisingly, there are few theatres. The **Teatro Guimerá** (www.teatroguimera.es) in Santa Cruz has been the mainstay for plays, musicals and the like since 1845. If cabaret-style shows are more your vibe then try Scandal (www.scandaldinnershow.com; charge) in Costa Adeje. It's a mix of burlesque, acrobatics and a gourmet dining experience.

Art lovers should make a beeline for **TEA Tenerife Espacio de las Artes** (www.teatenerife.es; free), where both permanent and visiting collections of modern art sit alongside what has to be one of the more beautiful libraries in the world. It also has an excellent gift shop featuring products by local artists.

Shopping

Many **designer shops** have outlets in the big resorts, but there is home-grown talent, too. Spain is known for its well-made and inexpensive **leather goods**, ranging from bags and belts to jackets and coats. Shoes in particular are relatively affordable and well designed.

A traditional Canarian costume

Embroidery and **lacemaking** are some of the traditional island crafts of Tenerife. Tablecloths and cushion covers with intricate patterns are a speciality. It is best to buy products from a shop, such as the Casa de los Balcones in La Orotava, or one of its six branches, rather than from a street seller.

Craft speciality shops include Artenerife (https://artenerife.com), which has several outlets across the island, including one in Casa de la Aduana in Puerto de la

Modern shopping centre in Playa de las Américas

Cruz, and one in Casa Torrehermosa in La Orotava. Lava rock and obsidian is used in **sculptures**, and a variety of **ceramics** are on sale. Pots are generally plain earthenware, many made in Guanche fashion. There are also copies of their fertility goddesses and die-stamps. At Los Calados in La Laguna (www.loscalados.es) you can purchase traditional Canarian dress.

Silver jewellery is worth a look, and **pearl** shops are a speciality. Tenerife Pearl (www.teneriferperla.com) has nine outlets and a main building with an exhibition at Armeñime on the main road between Adeje and Los Gigantes.

Cigars, hand-rolled from local tobacco, are also a good buy. Souvenirs include 50cm-long giant ones. Volcanic gravel impregnated with perfume is a novelty – roll the cigar in it before smoking to sweeten the aroma of the fumes.

Local **wines**, hard to find abroad, make great souvenirs. A good place to buy bottles from is the Casa del Vino at El Sauzal or directly from vineyards. Tenerife **honey** (*miel*) comes in various guises; there are handmade signs for the treasured produce along the roadside.

The best is from Las Cañadas del Teide – made from bees that suck the nectar of Teide broom. Other groceries to bring home might include jars of red or green *mojo* (see page 108), *bienmesabe* (see page 109) or cactus, papaya and other island preserves. All can be found in the shops and stalls of La Recova market in Santa Cruz.

Nightlife

Much of Tenerife's nightlife takes place on the streets. There are often spontaneous gatherings in the squares and on the beaches, and music and revellers spill out onto the pavements from bars.

In tourist hotspots there are plenty of clubs, as well as concerts. Little of the activity starts before midnight. As might be expected, **Playa de las Américas** has the most lavish after-dark scene on the island. Veronica's is the best-known strip, with around a hundred bars and clubs that keep going until dawn. Some of the most extravagant shows are at Pirámide de Arona.

The Castillo San Miguel (www.medievaladventure.com), signposted off the *autopista sur* at San Miguel,

NOTES

Bargaining is expected in the flea markets and at streetside stalls run by the North African merchants, but beware of 'special offers' from these traders, whose goods may include ivory jewellery or leather or fur goods from endangered species. Not only will you be supporting the killing of rare animals, but importing such items into Europe and the US is subject to heavy penalties.

The Santa Cruz Carnaval is one of the most lavish in Europe

has medieval nights. In **Costa Adeje** Papagayo Beach Club (www.papagayobeachclub.com), is a stylish venue with live bands, DJs and an open deck for watching the sunset.

Café de Paris at Avenida de Colón is a restaurant with dancing that attracts a slightly older crowd. Head for **Santa Cruz** for vibrant Spanish nightlife or hip bars in the Noria district or on Avenida de Anaga. **La Laguna** has a busy and youthful scene thanks to its large student population.

Festivals

Fiestas (festivals) are a huge part of island life, and there is a fair chance of seeing festivities during any stay – thirty days a year are officially set aside for events, based on the church calendar (see page 105).

Carnaval

Undoubtedly the most spectacular festival in the Canary Islands is the pre-Lent carnival, which is said to rival Rio. Fired by a Latin American fervour, it demands the same great lengths of preparation, and Puerto de la Cruz and Santa Cruz are both swallowed up by a series of events lasting nearly a fortnight.

The festival starts with the election of a Carnival Queen and ends in a big finale on Shrove Tuesday with the *coso*, a grand parade of floats and colourfully dressed participants. There is a strong drag element, and dancers are accompanied by *murgas*, groups singing satirical songs.

The shindig draws to a close on Ash Wednesday with El Entierro de la Sardina (the burial of the sardine), a mock funeral attended by people in outrageous outfits, who beat their breasts and shed crocodile tears.

The epic Corpus Christi festival

Corpus Christi

One of the most widely celebrated religious festivals on the island is the eight days (Octavo) of Corpus Christi at the end of May or the beginning of June. The best places to witness celebrations are La Laguna and La Orotava, where pavements are carpeted with spectacular displays of flowers and colourful volcanic sand.

The street procession that makes its way over them crushes the petals and scents the air with a sweet perfume.

Romerías

Corpus Christi marks the beginning of the Romería season of local festivals involving food, wine and dancing. A *romería* was originally a type of short annual pilgrimage; the word comes from a term that means 'a person travelling to Rome'. Nowadays, it is La Orotava and La Laguna that put on the biggest shows, with, respectively, the Romería de San Isidro in mid-June and the Romería de San Benita a fortnight later. Arico, Granadilla, Güímar and Icod also have large Romerías during the month.

Romería in Tegueste

Assumption

The biggest pilgrimage takes place on the day of the Assumption (15 August) at Candelaria, where the statue of Our Lady of Candelaria, patron saint of the Canary Islands, is paraded in the streets. On the day before, there is a re-enactment of the appearance of the Virgin to the Guanche shepherds.

Children wearing traditional dress at a local fiesta

Festivals and events

For public holidays, see page 136.

January: *Cabalgata de los Reyes* (Procession of the Three Kings, Santa Cruz and Garachico), with costumes, brass bands and camel cavalcades.

February/March: *Carnaval*, Santa Cruz's extravaganza; also in Puerto de la Cruz.

March/April: *Semana Santa* (Holy Week): solemn pre-Easter processions in many towns and cities throughout the island.

April: local fiestas on 25th (Icod, Tegueste).

May: spring festivals, opera festival (Santa Cruz). Fiestas de la Cruz (all places with Cruz [cross] in their name): processions, festivities and fireworks. Festival of San Isidro and Santa María de la Cabeza (Los Realejos and La Orotava): celebrations and large firework display. *Fiesta de Corpus Christi* (late May or early June, in La Laguna, La Orotava and elsewhere): beautiful flower carpets.

June: *Romería de San Isidro* (Tacoronte), *Romería de San Benito* (La Laguna): ox-drawn carts laden with local produce. Local fiestas (Arico, El Sauzal, Granadilla, Güímar, Icod).

July: *Fiesta de la Virgen del Carmen*, patron saint of seamen. *Romerías de Santiago Apóstol* (Festival of St James, Santa Cruz): pilgrimage, fireworks. Local fiestas (Candelaria, La Laguna, Los Realojos, Santiago del Teide).

August: *Fiesta de la Asunción* (Assumption, Candelaria): re-enactment of the appearance of the Blessed Virgin to the Guanches. Local fiestas (Garachico, Los Cristianos).

September: *Fiestas del Santísimo Cristo* (La Laguna, Tacaronte): floats, fireworks, sports, theatre and poetry. *Fiestas de Nuestra Señora de las Mercedes de Rojas* (El Médano in Granadilla): honours patron saint. Grape harvest. Local festivals (Güímar, Guía de Isora).

October: Wine tasting festival in Icod, La Orotava and Puerto de la Cruz, involving street parades, food and, of course, lots of wine. Local fiesta (Granadilla).

November: *Fiesta de San Andrés* (also known as *La Fiesta del Cacharro y la Castaña*) held in Puerto de la Cruz.

December: *Navidad* (Christmas). *Noche Vieja* (New Year's Eve).

Local in traditional costume drinking wine at a festival in La Orotava

Food and drink

Over the past decade, Tenerife has undergone a gourmet revolution with high-end restaurants scooping top international awards, and a generation of homegrown chefs championing Canarian produce and cuisine. There is still no shortage of restaurants serving chicken, chips and pizza in the resorts, but there is little excuse these days not to find great local food and drink.

Tenerife wines have also really started to grow again in popularity, in part due to the work done by winemaker Jonatan García Lima, of Suertes del Marqués, in preserving indigenous grape varieties and traditional methods, and putting them on the global wine map. Most good bars and restaurants now list Canarian wine on their menus.

Gofio escaldón

The trend of 'Nuevo Canario' (New Canarian) cuisine shows no signs of abating as chefs experiment with the islands' bountiful produce from *mar y montaña* (sea and mountains), prioritise sustainable practices and put a new spin on Canarian classics.

Top 10 things to try

1. Papas arrugadas con mojo

Potatoes are one of the mainstays of Tenerife, and

Papas arrugadas, or 'wrinkled' potatoes

the fact that they are called *papas* here, as they are in South America, and not *patatas*, as they are in Spain, is a clue to their affinities. There are no blights known to the local tuber, and there is a dozen regularly grown Andean varieties, notably *papa negra*, black potatoes. The size of squash balls and the colour of wood ash, they are usually prepared *arrugadas* or 'wrinkled', boiled in their jackets in highly salted water (traditionally seawater) and usually served with *mojo* sauce.

Mojo also accompanies both fish and meat dishes, and is made of olive oil, herbs and spices and comes in two colours – red and green. These are either poured on to a dish or served in their own bowls. The red *mojo picón* is spiked with dried peppers, chilli or paprika; the green *mojo verde* is flavoured with parsley or, more distinctly, coriander (*cilantro*). *Papas arrugadas* and *mojo* are ubiquitous across Tenerife, often favoured over chips or other sorts of potatoes.

2. Gofio

Wherever you eat on the island, it won't be long before you encounter *gofio*, the staple food of the Guanches. This is toasted ground corn, generally maize, but sometimes barley or wheat or even chickpeas, and it is served in a variety of ways. Grandmothers will mix it with hot milk for breakfast to make children 'big and strong'. It's often stirred into hot fish – or meat – stock to create a savoury dish called *gofio escaldón* or *escaldado*. Sometimes, it's kneaded with bananas or honey and almonds and sliced into rounds known as *pella gofio*. You'll also see it flavour ice cream, mousses, cheese and many other products.

3. Cheese

The Canaries are famous for their cheesemaking, particularly goat's cheese. You'll find many *queserías* (dairies) around Tenerife, some offering tours such as Quesería Montesdeoca (www.quesosmontesdeoca.com), where you can learn the process and

FISH ON THE MENU

Many of the exotic Atlantic shellfish listed on the extensive menus in Tenerife are unlike any you will see in most of Spain, and some are not easily translated. These include:

Abadejo – pollack; *aguja azul* – blue marlin; *bacalao* – cod; *chipirón* – baby squid; *caballa* – horse mackerel; *cabrilla* – comber; *cherne* – wreckfish; *choco* – cuttlefish; *congrio* – conger eel; *burro* – donkey fish; *corvina* – stone bass; *dorada* – gilthead bream; *lapas* – limpets; *lenguado* – sole; *merluza* – hake; *mero* – grouper; *morena* – moray eel; *pez espada* – swordfish; *rodaballo* – turbot; *salema* – gold-lined bream; *salmonete* – red mullet; *sama* – dentex; *sarda* – mackerel; *sargo* – white bream; *vieja* – parrot fish.

A typical Canarian roasted sea fish

taste the bounty. Cheese also appears on lots of menus, often *asado* (griddled) or *frito* (fried) and served with *mojos* and *miel de palma* (palm honey).

4. Cherne encebollado

One of the classic fish dishes of the Canaries, *cherne encebollado* celebrates this wonderful local fish that, when cooked, looks and tastes a little like cod. The recipe includes garlic, onions and peppers, with a white wine and paprika sauce.

5. Ropa vieja

Ropa vieja translates as 'old clothes' but don't let that put you off. It's a rich chickpea stew with pulled meat, potatoes, onions and peppers, flavoured with bay, saffron and parsley. It's a hearty meal and often served at the pop-up *guachinche* restaurants at wine harvest time.

6. Conejo al salmorejo

Rabbit has been one of the staple meats of the archipelago for centuries and '*al salmorejo*' is the most common way to serve it. The Canarian *salmorejo* has nothing to do with the Spanish cold tomato soup of the same name. Here, it is a white or red wine marinade and sauce made with garlic, oregano, chilli and paprika, in which the rabbit is slow cooked until the meat is meltingly tender. Try it at *El Calderito de la Abuela* (www.elcalderitodelaabuela.net) in Santa Úrsula in the north of Tenerife.

7. Bananas

You can't travel far in Tenerife without seeing a banana plantation. Look for the telltale large green leaves peeking out over the top of breeze-block farm walls. Bananas were the lifeblood of the island for decades before tourism descended, and it's due to the quantity of the fruit exported to the UK from the islands that London's Canary Wharf gets its name. Canarian bananas are smaller and sweeter than most other varieties and they are used in all sorts of ways. At fine-dining

Wine in traditional bottles

Restaurante Haydée by Víctor Suárez in Santa Cruze, the skins are even made into kimchi.

8. Wine

"O knight, thou lackest a cup of canary," says Sir Toby Belch in Shakespeare's *Twelfth Night*. He's likely referring to the wine once made in La Orotava that was hugely popular several centuries ago. Tenerife wine is thankfully growing in popularity again, as the island's native grape varieties and fertile volcanic soil produce incredibly interesting styles. Grapes to look out for are *listán negro* (sour cherry, raspberries and black pepper), *tintilla* (black fruits, chocolate and liquorice), *marmajuelo* (melon and grapefruit) and classic Malvasía (citrus and tropical fruit).

Barraquito, a next-level coffee

9. Barraquito

Barraquito takes coffee to the next level – both for the palate and the eyes. Served in a small narrow glass, this pick-me-up drink has layers of condensed milk, vanilla-flavoured Licor 43, espresso, hot milk, milk foam, a dusting of cinnamon and a twist of lemon peel. Marvel at the rainbow of colours before stirring it all together and taking a sip.

You'll find *barraquito* at cafés and restaurants across the island but try the version at *Palmelita* (www.palmelita.es) in Santa Cruz.

Tapas topped with red and white fish, lemon and parsley

10. Ron miel

It's said that Christopher Columbus took sugar cane from the Canaries to the Caribbean where rum was first made. But it didn't take long for the spirit to catch on in Tenerife, and rum production has flourished here for over a century. The local tipple is *ron miel*, or honey rum, a sweet, dark amber nectar. If you're asked at the end of a meal if you'd like a '*chupito*' – a shot of something as a digestif – make it a *ron miel*.

Where to eat

You'll find great places for food and drink right across the island, and while traditionally the north has been the gastronomic centre, the south has transformed over the past few years with a burgeoning restaurant scene that's home to some of Tenerife's most high-end dining spots.

Traditional tavern in La Laguna

Fine dining

Most of the Michelin-starred and haute-cuisine restaurants can be found in the luxury hotels of the south. *Nub* (www.nubrestaurante.com) at *Gran Hotel Bahía del Duque* stands out from the crowd for its clash of culinary titans, with husband-and-wife team Andrea and Fernanda bringing together the best of their home countries of Italy and Chile, respectively. The legendary *El Rincón de Juan Carlos* (www.elrincondejuancarlos.com) by Tenerife's own Padrón brothers is another gourmand big-hitter.

Bars and tascas

You'll find bars, *tascas* and *bodegas* clustered in every town and peppered along roads throughout the island. Often, they are casual family-run places dishing up a selection of Canarian food

EATING OUT ETIQUETTE

Tinerfeños tend to gulp down a quick coffee and something sweet first thing and then eat something more substantial at around 11am, perhaps a *croissant mixto* (with ham and cheese). Lunch is the main meal of the day, taken around 2 or 3pm, and is usually hearty. *Merienda* (afternoon tea) comes at around 5pm, and then dinner from 9pm. Bars open late into the night and clubs even later if you plan on going out afterwards. Many restaurants close on Sunday night and one day a week, often Monday. On the whole, dining is casual unless it's a fine-dining restaurant and, even then, it's not usually formal, though you will find that *Tinerfeños* like to dress up anyway.

and other tapas. While menus might be split into small plates (*enyesques*) and mains, there's no need to order this way and you can ask for everything to arrive together to share. Cool little restaurants proliferate in Santa Cruz and La Laguna. *Tinerfeños* live their lives outside, and most places will spill out onto the street or have terrace tables. Look out for those offering a *menú del día* – a good-value set menu option that usually includes wine and coffee in the price.

Guachinches

Guachinches are informal pop-up restaurants that you'll find mainly in the north of the island from around October to March. They were originally thought up by winemakers to sell their surplus wine. Barns, garages and sheds are all used for these makeshift cafeterias. There are strict regulations on *guachinches*, which can only open for a maximum of three months a year. They typically serve simple Canarian fare and their own wine to patrons on plastic patio furniture. Remember to bring cash as some don't take card. Often, they are only signposted with handwritten signs on the side of the road.

To help you order

Could we have a table, please? **¿Nos puede dar una mesa, por favor?**
Do you have a set menu? **¿Tiene un menú del día?**
The menu, please **La carta, por favor**
I would like... **Quisiera...**
The bill, please **La cuenta, por favor**

Menu reader

agua mineral mineral water
a la plancha grilled
al ajillo in garlic
almejas clams
al punto/medio medium
arroz rice
asado roast
atún tuna
azúcar sugar
bacalao cod
bocadillo sandwich
boquerones anchovies
bien hecho well done
buey/res beef
café coffee
calamares squid
cangrejo crab
cerdo pork
cerveza beer
champiñones mushrooms
chorizo cured sausage
cocido stew
cordero lamb
ensalada salad
entremeses/enyesques hors-d'oeuvre
gambas prawns
helado ice cream
jamón serrano cured ham
judías beans
langosta lobster
leche milk
mariscos shellfish
mejillones mussels
pan bread
pescado fish
picante spicy
poco hecho rare
pollo chicken
postre dessert
pulpo octopus
queso cheese
sal salt
ternera veal
tortilla omelette
salsa/mojo sauce
vino wine
verduras vegetables

Places to eat

Each restaurant and café reviewed in this Guide is accompanied by a price category, based on the cost of a three-course meal (or similar) for one, including wine, cover and service:

€€€€ = over €50
€€€ = €40–50
€€ = €25–40
€ = under €25

The northeast

Anaga

Cruz del Carmen Las Mercedes Km6. An ideal stop, by the Cruz del Carmen *mirador*, when exploring the Anaga Hills. Solid Canarian cooking, with both meat and fish soups and home-made sweets, in three spacious dining rooms. **€€**

San Cristobal de La Laguna

Arepera Punto Criollo Calle El Tizón 6. One of the best traditional restaurants, famous for its *gofio* and *arepas* (filled Venezuelan flatbread). A perfect location in the old part of La Laguna. **€**

Restaurante Guaydil Calle Dean Palahi, 26, www.restauranteguaydil.com. Hugely popular, atmospheric restaurant in the heart of La Laguna, serving interesting twists on classic tapas. It has an extensive gluten-free menu. **€€**

Taberna Santo Domingo Calle Santo Domingo 24, www.santodomingo24.com. A *tasca* known for its selection of hams and cheeses, as well as meats and seafood – try the octopus or the *secreto Ibérico* (pork fillet). Good local wines at moderate prices. **€€**

La Tasca de Cristian Calle Marques de Celada 17, www.latascadecristian.es. Warm and welcoming, this cosy haunt serves up delicious meat and seafood dishes. There's a good selection of wines and the service is excellent. **€€**

Tasca la Comarca Camino de San Miguel de Geneto 147. Unattractive as it may seem from the outside, this small restaurant and bar serves excellent food, including a wide selection of tapas typical in the Spanish region of Asturias. Make sure you leave space (and the portions are big) for a dessert; the *arroz con leche* is excellent. **€€**

Los Naranjeros

Restaurante El Empedrado Carretera General del Norte 284, www.empedrado.es. Set in an old house, this is one of many popular restaurants between La Laguna and Tacoronte that fill up with diners at weekend lunchtimes. The house speciality is grilled meat plated in generous portions: chicken, pork, veal, rabbit, lamb, goat, but the *cochino negro canario* is particularly recommended. Good value for money. **€€**

Santa Cruz

El Aguila Plaza del Chicharro, www.elaguilarestaurante.com. This restaurant spills out onto a central pedestrian square with plenty for diners to watch – including a large outdoor screen screening the big football games. Pick from the huge array of tapas or large *parillas* (grills) of fish or meat – simply head up to the counter and point to whatever takes your fancy. **€€**

Colmado 1917 Calle Dr. Jose Naveiras 38, www.colmado1917.com. Very cool tasting bar inside the iconic *Grand Mencey Hotel*. Chefs rustle together dishes with minimal intervention, cleverly shining a light on the fresh, local products. Wine pairings are all local. **€€€**

Gastrobar Cortxo Plaza de Ireneo Gonzalez 5, www.cortxo.com. Fabulous little wine and tapas bar with a huge list of bottles, including local, national and international labels. There are very few seats inside, but the terrace in the pretty square is where most of the action happens. The atmosphere is lovely, especially in the evenings. **€€**

El Gusto por el Vino Avenida San Sebastían 55, www.elgustoporelvino.com. A decent tapas restaurant and wine bar opened by the biggest local wine distributor. Short but well-executed menu featuring all the usual classics. **€**

La Hierbita Calle El Clavel 19, www.lahierbita.es. Located in a delightful old house with a string of small rooms spread across two floors, *La Hierbita* serves home-cooked cuisine from popular Canarian recipes. Try *almagrote gomero*, a rich cheese paste from La Gomera, Canarian stew or grilled fish, and end with freshly made dessert washed down with a shot of La Hierbita, a traditional liqueur. **€€**

Palmelita Calle del Castillo 9, www.palmelita.es. Wonderful café and bakery situated on the main street in Santa Cruz. It serves top-notch coffee and home-made pastries as well as freshly prepared sandwiches with seasonal fillings. Snag a seat outside to watch the comings and goings of the city. **€**

La Posada del Pez Carretera Taganana 2, San Andrés. A small, cosy and truly excellent seafood restaurant near the Playa de las Teresitas. The *mar y montaña* (sea and mountain) – a mix of fish and oxtail on one plate – is worth a try. **€€**

Taberna Ramón Rambla de Santa Cruz 56, www.tabernaramon.com. A typical *taberna* with a lively ambience, and pork legs hanging from the ceiling. Order a selection of tapas to share and scores of different wines; you'll want to sample as many as you can. **€€**

The north

El Sauzal

Casa del Vino Autopista General del Norte Km21, www.casadelvino tenerife.com. The restaurant in this elegant seventeenth-century estate, now occupied by the wine museum, serves contemporary Canarian food, and is the best place to try – and seek advice about – Canarian wines. There is also a more casual *tasca* bar with views from its terrace down to the sea. **€€€**

Restaurante Casa Odon Carretera General del Norte km 21. Traditional restaurant dedicated to authentic Canarian cuisine. The portions are abundant, the food delicious and the service quick and efficient. The mushroom plates are highly recommended. Excellent value for money. **€€**

Icod de los vinos

El Mortero Calle San Sebastián 7, www.restauranteelmortero.com. The food in this restaurant is creative, abundant and excellent quality. The traditional menu changes every six months and is based on seasonal produce, ensuring that all ingredients are deliciously fresh. A bit pricey, but definitely worth a try. **€€**

Santa Úrsula

El Calderito de la Abuela Carretera Provincial 130, www.elcalderito delaabuela.net. A well-known, great-value restaurant that's been in same family for three generations. It serves some of the best examples of traditional Canarian food; don't miss the *conejo al salmorejo* (marinated rabbit). Nearby, the same family also runs *Donde Mario* and *La Bodeguita de Enfrente*, which are also worth a visit. **€€**

La Orotava

Bar Los Castillos Calle Cologan 10, www.barloscastillos.es. Small, rustic, family-run restaurant offering typical Canarian dishes such as cuttlefish, *cherne* (wreckfish), squid in its own ink and rabbit stew. There's a friendly atmosphere and the staff are helpful. **€**

Sabor Canario Calle Carrera Escultor Estevez 17. This old townhouse in La Orotava's historic centre dates from 1580. The dishes are traditional too, including rabbit in *salmorejo* sauce, and various manifestations of *gofio*. It also has a good selection of wines. **€€**

Victoria Hermano Apolinar 8, www.hotelruralvictoria.com. Beautifully located on an indoor patio at the heart of La Orotava's old town. Daily *menu del día* for around €15, which includes a starter, main, dessert and glass of wine (or coffee/juice). **€€**

Puerto de la Cruz

Meson El Monasterio Carretera La Montañeta 12, Los Realejos, www.mesonelmonasterio.com. This former monastery enjoys stunning views from its terraces and gardens. Four different restaurants cater for all tastes, whether it's *carnes a la piedra* (meat cooked on a hot stone), seafood specialities, Canarian and Spanish cuisine or a plate of tapas. The *bodega* has a wide selection of wines, and the on-site shop stocks hams, salami, olives and cheeses. **€€**

The Oriental Avenida Richard J. Yeoward, https://hotelbotanico.com. Located within the *Hotel Botánico, The Oriental* specialises in Thai cookery with pan-Asian touches. The ambiance is formal. **€€€**

Régulo Calle Pérez Zamora 16. One of the best restaurants in Puerto de la Cruz, *Régulo* occupies an eighteenth-century Canarian house with balconies around a delightful patio. Specialities of the house include *lapas a la plancha* (grilled limpets) and *solomillo relleno de camembert* (fillet steak stuffed with camembert). **€€€**

Slow Coffee Tenerife Calle Pérez Zamora, www.slowcoffeetenerife.com. Trendy café and coffee shop serving expertly made brews. An ideal place to grab a takeaway first thing in the morning and wander the sunny streets or promenade of Puerto de la Cruz. **€**

Tasca El Olivo Calle Iriarte 1, www.tascaelolivo.eatbu.com. A bright *taverna* with a menu featuring Canarian and Spanish staples, including *papas arrugadas* and tortilla, pork loins, fresh local fish and generous portions of seafood. Vegetarian options are available – try the braised vegetables - and there's a fine selection of local wines and international beers. **€€**

Tegueste

Casa Tomás Camino del Portezuelo 2, www.restaurantecasatomas.com. Home-made Canarian food, with dishes including *piñas con costilla* (spareribs with potatoes and corn cobs). Busy at weekends. **€€**

Mesón El Drago Calle Marqués de Celada 2, www.dragogamonal.com. Family-run, award-winning establishment serving some of the best Canarian dishes in Tenerife. Delicious culinary creations include watercress soup with yams and red onion, cheese and *gofio*. Special menu for children. **€€€**

The northwest

Garachico

Anturium in Hotel San Roque Calle Esteban de Ponte 32, www.restauranteanturium.com. A mix of Canarian and Mediterranean cuisine, with delicacies such as wrinkled potatoes with Canarian *mojos* and *almogrote* or tagliatelle with smoked cheese, sauce and basil. Great selection of wines. **€€€**

Gaía de Isora

M.B. *The Ritz-Carlton Tenerife*, Abama, www.mb-tenerife.com. The signature restaurant of Basque chef Martín Berasategui (hence the name), renowned for inspirational Mediterranean cuisine. The restaurant has been awarded two Michelin stars, so expect gourmet fare (and correspondingly steep prices). **€€€€**

Masca

Restaurante "El Guanche" Alte Schule Calle El Lomito. A delightful setting, looking down over the *barranco* (valley), with a shady terrace full of flowers. Serves local food and has an extensive vegan menu. **€€**

The south

Chayofa

La Finca Chayofa Calle Taroso. Situated between Playa de las Américas and Arona, this former tomato-packing factory functions as an art gallery for local talent as well as a café and bistro. Good to drop by any time of day; it livens up on Sundays with a jazz brunch. **€€**

Los Abrigos

Restaurante Los Abrigos Calle La Marina 3, www.restaurantelosabrigos.com. Wonderful portside restaurant with extensive menu of fish, from *abadejo* (pollack) to *vieja* (parrotfish). Crowded at weekends. The next door *Perlas de Mar* has a similarly fantastic seafood offering. **€€€**

Los Cristianos

Gran Cafè Tenerife Avenida Los Playeros. Beachfront café serving snacks and coffee with views of the Los Cristianos port. Good for breakfast and a pick-me-up brew. **€**

Habibi Avenida de la Habana, www.restaurantehabibilasvistas.es. Tourists enjoy this cheap and cheerful touch of Lebanon on the island. Offers great views, especially at sunset, and delicious food. Service is very efficient. **€€**

El Sol Chez Jacques Paseo Roma, Los Cristianos. Opened in 1974, *El Sol Chez Jacques* is one of the oldest restaurants in Tenerife, serving classic French fare including a superb beef bourguignon with six home-made sauces to choose from. **€€€**

Playa de Las Américas

First Love Paseo Tarajal, Centro Commercial Compostela Beach. This small, unpretentious Italian haunt is a gem, serving home-made pasta dishes. The friendly owners make the meal even more enjoyable. The menu of Italian classics is rather short; the salads are especially delicious. **€€**

Mesón Las Lanzas Avenida Noelia Afonso Cabrera. It's not easy to find an authentic Spanish restaurant in this very touristic part of the island. This one is rather expensive, but worth paying for. The decor is traditional Spanish – and so is the menu. Great choice of seafood and excellent wines. **€€€€**

Molino Blanco Avenida Austria 5, www.molino-blanco.com. Charcoal grills and wood-fired ovens are the main calling card here, with chefs plating up such delights as suckling lamb, goat meat and oxtail stew as well as fresh fish. An animated atmosphere bubbles throughout its three dining rooms, with live music performances, and the landmark white windmill makes it easy to find. **€€€€**

Taste 1973 *Hotel Villa Cortés*, www.europe-hotels.org. Chef Diego Schattenhofer delves into Tenerife's gastronomic history at this fine-dining restaurant. There are two tasting menus to choose from, with optional wine parings. No under-12s. **€€€€**

San Isidro

Mesón de Antonio Calle Cuevas de Cho Portada. Decent spot, located just off the town, offering excellent meat dishes. Great service. **€€**

The southwest

Adeje

Otelo 1 Calle Los Molinos, Barranco del Infierno, www.otelorestaurante.com. At the entrance to the dramatic Barranco del Infierno gorge, this unpretentious bar-restaurant is popular with hikers. The main dishes are rabbit or crispy garlic chicken, best washed down with local wine. **€€**

Costa Adeje

Donaire *GF Victoria*, www.restaurantedonaire.com**.** With fabulous views over the sea and Costa Adeje from its top-floor perch in the *GF Victoria* hotel, *Donaire* is the brainchild of chef Jesús Camacho who puts a modern take on classic Canarian dishes and ingredients. It scored a Michelin star in 2025. **€€€€**

Nub Bahia del Duque, www.nubrestaurante.com. Chefs Andrea Bernardi and Fernanda Fuentes-Cárdenas helm the kitchen of this Michelin-starred restaurant, combining to create a unique mix of Canarian and European cuisine. Formal dress required; no under-12s. **€€€€**

Restaurante Haydée by Víctor Suárez *Gran Tacande Hotel*, www.restaurantehaydee.rest. Chef Víctor Suárez, the eleventh winner of the prestigious Absolute Regional Championship of Cooks in the Canary Islands, draws his culinary inspiration not only from the archipelago but also other parts of the world, especially Southeast Asia. And it's paid off: *Restaurante Haydée* was awarded a Michelin star in 2023. **€€€€**

La Caleta

Il Bocconcino by Royal Hideaway *Royal Hideaway Corales Suites*, www.gastrocorales.com. Italian haute-cuisine by chef Niki Pavanelli. It scooped a Michelin star in 2025 but doesn't feel stuffy or overly formal. Attire is smart-casual, so no sports, beach or pool wear. **€€€€**

Masía del Mar Calle El Muelle 3, www.masiadelmargroup.com. This great harbourside fish restaurant offers a real flavour of the Tenerife coast. Set in a restored warehouse dating from 1568, it serves some of the freshest seafood and most authentic dishes available on the coast. **€€**

Restaurante Celso Calle El Cabezo 24, www.restaurantecelso.com. Superb fish restaurant perched on the edge of the rock with far-reaching views. Very popular so book ahead or prepare to wait with a drink. **€€**

SEEN by Olivier *Tivoli La Caleta*, www.seenbyolivier.com/Tenerife. A very cool and trendy restaurant in the equally chic *Tivoli La Caleta* hotel. Expect Canarian food with an international flair, live music and views of the sea and neighbouring La Gomera. Come for sunset – and sundowers. **€€€**

Travel essentials

Practical information

Accessible travel 128
Accommodation 128
Airports 129
Apps 129
Bicycle rental 129
Budgeting for your trip 130
Camping 130
Car hire 131
Climate 131
Crime 131
Customs and entry requirements 132
Driving 132
Electricity 133
Embassies and consulates 133
Emergencies 134
Getting to Tenerife 134
Health and medical care 135
Holidays 136
Language 136
LGBTQ+ travellers 137
Lost property 137
Money matters 137
Opening hours 138
Police 138
Public transport 139
Taxis 140
Telephones 140
Time difference 140
Tipping 141
Toilets 141
Tourist information 141
Websites 141

Accessible travel

Tenerife is well adapted to the needs of travellers with additional accessibility needs. Airports, accommodation and the major resorts are generally set up for wheelchair-users and those with limited mobility. Los Cristianos is just one of at least fourteen beaches with accessible facilities, including parking, changing huts and toilets, and amphibious wheelchairs. There are wheelchair trails in both Parque Nacional del Teide and Parque Rural Anaga. Limitless Travel (www.limitlesstravel.org) in the UK offers holidays for disabled travellers.

Wheelchairs and mobility scooters can be hired from Canarian Mobility (www.canarianmobility.com), Orange Badge (www.orangebadge.eu) or LeRo (www.lero.es).

Accommodation

Most hotels and apartments are concentrated in the main towns and resorts, particularly in the south of the island. The standard of accommodation is generally high, with a large number of luxury resorts. Styles vary from contemporary design to traditional Canarian houses, country houses (*casas rurales*) to country estates (*fincas*). Package tourism predominates but there are a growing number of hotels for independent travellers, especially in the quieter north.

Prices are reasonable by European standards and establishments are graded from one-star to five-star Gran Lujo (GL), which signifies top-of-the-range quality, though quality is not always directly reflected in price. Santa Cruz de Tenerife and Puerto de la Cruz have a selection of lower-rated places. By law, prices must be displayed in hotel receptions and in the rooms. Breakfast is not always included in the basic rate.

There are plenty of apartments, which are graded with one to three 'keys', shown with symbols, depending on their amenities. There are also aparthotels, often graded as hotels, where each room or suite has its own kitchen facilities yet retains all the trappings of a hotel.

If you are visiting during the more expensive high season (December, January, July and August), book accommodation well in advance and be aware that minimum stays in some hotels are three to five days. The official Tenerife website www.webtenerife.com gives details of around two hundred places to stay.

a single/double room with bath/shower **una habitación individual/doble con baño/ducha**
What's the rate per night? **¿Cuál es el precio por noche?**
Is breakfast included? **¿Está incluído el desayuno?**

Airports

There are two airports on the island. Most international flights use Reina Sofía Airport (Tenerife Sur) in the south at Granadilla de Abona, 11 miles (18km) east of Los Cristianos. Buses run to Los Cristianos and Playa de las Américas (about 25min) and to Puerto de la Cruz (1hr 40min).

Los Rodeos Airport (Tenerife Norte), near La Laguna, handles mainly interisland and Spanish air traffic. For general airport information, see www.aena.es.

Apps

Tenerife ON (www.tenerifeon.es) is a slick app that allows you to discover outdoor Tenerife, from walking trails to maps, and is run by the governmental Cabildo de Tenerife. Infoplayas (www.infoplayascanarias.es) from the Canary Islands government gives a comprehensive interactive list of beaches, including weather and facilities. Common taxi apps such as Uber, Sixt and NTaxi are available on the island, particularly in the south, while island bus company Titsa has a web-based app for route planning.

Bicycle rental

Cycling is a great way to explore the island but be prepared for hot and challenging rides in the mountainous areas. Cycling in Tenerife (www.cyclingintenerife.com) offers bike tours for all levels of fitness. See also Mr Bike (www.downhillbiketour.com) for downhill cycling tours. Bike Point

Tenerife (www.bikepointtenerife.com) is a one-stop shop that sells gear, rents bikes, offers cycling tours and provides repairs and servicing.

Budgeting for your trip

Here's a list of some average prices in euros.

Accommodation: Rates for a double room can range from as low as €35 at a *pensión* or *hostal* to as much as €400 at a top-of-the-range five-star hotel. A pleasant three-star stay will cost in the range of €90–€100. However, rates increase during the high season, beginning around late November and culminating with the Carnaval in February/March, and then again in July and August.

Apartments: For a family apartment, prices per night range from around €30 for one key to more than €80 for three keys. Discounts are often available for longer stays.

Attractions: Most museums and gardens charge a minimal entry fee of around €5. More expensive (€10–30) are the larger attractions such as the Pirámides de Güímar and theme parks.

Car hire: Around €35 a day.

Meals and drinks: In a bar, a continental breakfast will cost from €4. The cheapest three-course meal, **menú del día**, with one drink, in a small bar/restaurant, will be around €10–15. Dinner in a mid-range restaurant will likely be €30 per person, including wine.

Petrol: Around €0.95 a litre.

Sports: Golf green fees (per day) range from €45 up to €85 for 18 holes. Tennis court fees start at about €6 an hour, and horse riding starts at about €20 an hour.

Taxis: A taxi journey within a town is likely to cost €5–7. The fare from Playa de las Américas to Reina Sofia airport is around €35.

Camping

Camping is not a common option on the island, and it is prohibited in the national parks. There is a site on the south coast, *Camping Nauta Cañada Blanca* (www.campingnauta.es), in Las Galletas, 2km (1 mile) from the beach. Two other camping sites are *Punta del Hidalgo* in La Laguna and *Quimpi* (www.quimpi.com) in El Rosario.

Car hire (see also Driving)

To hire a car, you must be over 21, sometimes 25, and you will need your passport, a major credit card and a valid driving licence that you have held for at least twelve months. Cars are generally manual transmission.

There are around a hundred local car-hire outfits – 25 in Santa Cruz alone – and these tend to be cheaper than the better-known companies. It is also cheaper if you hire a car before you leave home, especially online. Local companies include CICAR (www.cicar.com), Auto Reisen (autoreisen.com), and Traditional Rent a Car (www.trc-cars.com). All the international behemoths (Avis, Europcar, Hertz) have offices at the airports and in the major towns.

I'd like to rent a car for one day/week. **Quisiera alquilar un coche por un día/una semana.**
Please include full insurance. **Haga el favor de incluir el seguro a todo riesgo.**

Climate

With the temperature a steady 22°C (72°F) year-round, sunshine is the rule, but the weather in the north and eastern parts of the island can be changeable. In spring there is a cold and wet gust from the northwest, and in autumn the famous hot *sirocco* raises the mercury. Tenerife is on a parallel with West Africa, and the temperatures in the southern resorts and in the *malpaís* can be high. Up in the hills, it is much cooler, even in La Laguna, and the trade winds keep the northeast of the island damp for most of the year. Temperatures drop to minus figures around El Teide's summit and in the Cañadas.

Crime

Tenerife does not have a high crime rate, and theft is only an issue in tourist areas. There is some opportunistic bag-snatching and pickpocketing in busy places such as markets or at fiestas, though. Never leave valuable items in your car; instead, stash them securely in the safe in your hotel room, including your passport. Burglaries of holiday apartments do occur, so keep doors and windows locked when you are out. Report all thefts to the local police within 24 hours for your own insurance purposes.

I want to report a theft. **Quiero denunciar un robo.**

Customs and entry requirements

Most visitors, including citizens of all EU countries, the UK, the US, Canada, Australia and New Zealand, require only a valid passport to enter Spain for stays of up to ninety days in any 180-day period. However, from late 2026, citizens from non-EU countries, including the UK, will need an ETIAS (European Travel Information and Authorization System) to enter Spain for short stays; visit https://travel-europe.europa.eu/etias_en for more information. Check before travelling as you will need to apply before you arrive in Spain.

Although Spain is in the EU, there is still a restriction on duty-free allowances at customs (*aduana*) when returning to the UK from the Canary Islands. This is: 200 cigarettes or 50 cigars or 250g smoking tobacco; 1-litre spirits over 22 percent or 2-litres under 22 percent, 4 litres of wine.

Driving

Driving conditions. Drive on the right, pass on the left, yield right-of-way to all vehicles coming from your right. Slow down when passing through villages and be aware that you may encounter anything from a herd of goats to large potholes.

Speed limits on the island are 120km/h (74mph) on motorways, 100km/h (62mph) on dual highways, 90km/h (52mph) on country roads, 50km/h (31mph) in built-up areas and 20km/h (13mph) in residential areas.

Motorways are toll-free. In the main towns traffic can be heavy and one-way systems confusing, as road signs are woefully inadequate.

Parking. You are more likely to find a parking space during lunch hours

(2–4pm). Consider parking at the edge of towns and taking buses or taxis to the centre.

Petrol. Petrol stations on main roads are often open 24 hours. However, they are less frequent off the beaten track and often close at night and on Sundays; plan ahead. Most hire cars take unleaded petrol, which in Spain is called *sin plomo*.

Traffic police. Civil guards (*guardia civil*) patrol the roads on black motorbikes. In towns the municipal police handle traffic control. If you are fined for a traffic offence, you will have to pay on the spot.

Seat belts are compulsory. Children up to the age of 12 and measuring less than 135cm in height must travel in an adequate child-restraint system. Using mobile phones or GPS devices while driving is illegal.

Road signs. Apart from the standard international pictographs you may encounter the following:

Aparcamiento Parking
Desviación Detour
Obras Road works
Peligro Danger
Senso unico One way
¿Se puede aparcar aqui? Can I park here?
Llénelo, por favor, con super. Fill the tank please, top grade.
Ha habido un accidente. There has been an accident.

Electricity

The standard supply is 220v with continental-style two-pin sockets. North American 110v appliances will need a transformer.

Embassies and consulates

Santa Cruz de Tenerife: **United Kingdom**: Plaza Weyler, 8, 1st Floor, tel: 928 26 25 08, access by appointment only. **Republic of Ireland (Honorary Consulate)**: C/Villalba Hervás 9–9º, Oficina 2, tel: 922 24 56 71 (call to find out current opening hours). The nearest **US** consulate is in Las Palmas, capital of neighbouring Gran Canaria, at Edificio Arca, Calle Los Martínez de Escobar 3, Oficina 7, tel: 928 27 12 59. It opens 10am–1pm weekdays. For other countries' representations, you may have to call Madrid.

If you lose your passport or run into trouble with the authorities or the police, contact your consulate for advice. Consulates can issue temporary passports for a fee; you will need an official statement of loss or theft from the police, plus two passport-size photographs.

Where is the American/ British consulate? **¿Dónde está el consulado americano/británico?**

Emergencies

The general emergency number is **112**. For the civil guard dial 062, for the local police dial 092, for the national police dial 091 and for an ambulance (Cruz Roja) 112/902 22 22 92.

There are the following hospitals in Tenerife:

Playa de las Americas: Hospiten Sur (www.hospiten.com).

Puerto de la Cruz: Hospiten Bellevue, Hospiten Tamaragua (www.hospiten.com).

Santa Cruz: Hospital Universitario de Canarias, Hospital Nuestra Señora de la Candelaria, and Hospiten Rambla.

Police **Policía**
Fire **Fuego**
Help! **¡Socorro!**
Stop! **¡Deténgase!**

Getting to Tenerife

By air: There are many flights from the UK to Tenerife. The flight time is 3h 30min–4hr 30min, and the cost £100–350. All-in package holidays can be the least expensive way to travel. British Airways (www.britishairways.com), and the national carrier Iberia (www.iberia.com) also have promotional deals in the UK.

There are no direct flights to Tenerife from the US. Airlines travel via major European airports, with Spanish state airline Iberia flying via Madrid, from where internal flights connect to all the Canary Islands. Flights can take 12–13hr and cost from $1000.

Interisland flights are available with Binter Canarias (www.bintercanarias.com) and Canaryfly (www.canaryfly.es).

By ship: Naviera Trasmediterránea (www.armastrasmediterranea.com) has a limited number of sailings from Cádiz and ferry connections with other Canary Islands.

Other ferry operators on Canary Islands include Fred Olsen (www.fredolsen.es) and Naviera Armas (www.navieraarmas.com).

Health and medical care

While tap water is safe to drink, it comes from desalination plants, so people generally opt for bottled water: *con gas* (sparkling) and *sin gas* (still). Remember that water is scarce, so don't waste it.

Non-EU visitors should take out private medical insurance. The UK Global Health Insurance Card (GHIC), which entitles British citizens to cheaper (or even free) healthcare, is available in the UK from post offices or online at www.services.nhsbsa.nhs.uk (if you have a valid European Health Insurance Card (EHIC), you can use it until it expires). Before being treated it is advisable to check that the doctor is working within the Spanish Health Service.

Dental treatment is not generally available under this system, so private insurance is strongly advised.

Farmacias (chemists/drugstores) can deal with a number of health problems. They are usually open during normal shopping hours. After hours, at least one pharmacy – the *farmacia de guardia* – per town remains open all night, and its location is posted in the window of all other *farmacias* nearby and printed in local newspapers. You can check the address of the nearest *farmacia de guardia* online at the website https://farmaciatenerife.com.

Where's the nearest (all-night) chemist? **¿Dónde está la farmácia (de guardia) más cercana?**
I need a doctor/dentist. **Necesito un médico/dentista.**
an upset stomach **molestias de estómago**
Is this service public or private? **¿Es este servicio público o privado?**

Holidays

In addition to these Spanish national holidays, many local and smaller religious and civic holidays are celebrated in various towns.

1 January *Año Nuevo* New Year's Day
6 January *Epifanía/Día de los Reyes Magos* Epiphany/Three Kings' Day
1 May *Día del Trabajo* Labour Day
30 May *Día de Canarias* Canary Islands Day
25 July *Santiago Apóstol* St James's Day
15 August *Asunción/Nuestra Señora de la Candelaria* Assumption
12 October *Día de la Hispanidad* Columbus Day
1 November *Todos los Santos* All Saints' Day
6 December *Día de la Constitución* Constitution Day
8 December *Inmaculada Concepción* Immaculate Conception
25 December *Navidad* Christmas Day
Movable dates:
Carnaval Week of Shrove Tuesday
Jueves Santo Maundy Thursday
Viernes Santo Good Friday
Corpus Christi Corpus Christi

Language

The official language of the Canary Islands is Spanish. However, Canarian

Spanish, which is the variant of standard Spanish spoken in the archipelago, is a little different from that of the mainland. For instance, islanders don't lisp when they pronounce the letters c or z. The language of the Canaries is spoken with a slight lilt, reminiscent of the Caribbean, and a number of 'New World' words are used. The most common are *guagua* (pronounced wah-wah), meaning bus, and *papa* (potato). In tourist areas German, English and some French is often spoken, or at least understood.

Do you speak English? **¿Habla usted inglés?**
I don't speak Spanish. **No hablo español.**

LGBTQ+ travellers

Tenerife is extremely safe and welcoming to the LGBTQ+ community, and while the scene here is not as big as neighbouring Gran Canaria, it is growing. ARN – Culture & Business Pride takes place each December in Playa de las Américas. You'll find the majority of LGBTQ+ bars and accommodation options in the south. Check out www.visitlgbtq.com and www.travelgay.com for further information.

Lost property

If you lose an item, report the loss to the Municipal Police or the Guardia Civil (see Police) and retain a copy of their report for insurance purposes.

I've lost my wallet/pocketbook/passport. **He perdido mi cartera/bolso/pasaporte.**

Money matters

Currency. The monetary unit in the Canary Islands is the euro (€). Bank notes are available in denominations of 500, 200, 100, 50, 20, 10 and 5. The euro is subdivided into 100 cents and there are coins available for €1 and €2 and for 50, 20, 10, 5, 2 and 1 cent.

Currency exchange. Banks are the best place to exchange currency as they tend to have the best exchange rates. *Casas de cambio* (exchange offices) stay open outside banking hours. Most larger hotels will also change guests' money, but the rate is less favourable than at the bank. Always take your passport when you go to change money.

Credit cards. Major cards (Visa/Eurocard/MasterCard, etc) are widely recognised on Tenerife, although some smaller businesses prefer cash. Credit and debit cards are also useful for obtaining cash from ATMs, which are found in all towns and resorts, and will usually give you the best exchange rate. Prepaid currency cards are also worth considering, as they may help you to avoid high bank fees when making payments at shops and restaurants.

Where's the nearest bank (currency exchange office)? **¿Dónde está el banco (la oficina de cambio) más cercano/a?**

I want to change some dollars/pounds. **Quiero cambiar dólares/libras esterlinas.**

Do you accept travellers' cheques? **¿Acepta usted cheques de viajero?**

Can I pay with this credit card? **¿Puedo pagar con esta tarjeta de crédito?**

Opening hours

Some shops, offices and other businesses observe the afternoon siesta, opening from Monday to Saturday 10am–1.30 pm and 5–8.30pm (some on Saturday morning only). In tourist areas most places stay open all day. Post offices are usually open 8.30–2pm; banks 8am–2pm Mon–Fri, with some also open on the occasional afternoon or Saturday morning from Oct–June; shopping malls 9.30am–10pm.

Police

There are three police forces in Tenerife, as there are in the rest of Spain. The *guardia civil* (civil guard) is the oldest and the primary force in Spain, and is technically made up of military officers as opposed to police. Each town also has its own *policía municipal* (municipal police), whose uniform varies depending on the town and season but is mostly a combination of blue and grey. The third force, the *cuerpo nacional de policía*, is a national anti-crime unit whose officers wear a dark-navy uniform. All police officers are armed.

Where is the nearest police station? **¿Dónde está la comisaría más cercana?**

Public transport

Airlines: A number of airlines fly between the islands and are not much more expensive than ferries, though it is not such an eco-friendly way to travel. Binter Canarias (www.bintercanarias.com) runs the most frequent services.

Bus services: Buses (*guaguas*) are run by Titsa (Transporte Interurbanos de Tenerife SA; www.titsa.com) and are regular, fast and cheap. They cover all major and most minor destinations on the island. Tickets can be bought on board, but if you buy a BonoVía card from newsagents, bus stations or some shops beforehand, you benefit from up to half-price travel on all routes. Timetables can be obtained at bus depots, tourist offices or online.

Tram services: The tram service connecting Santa Cruz and La Laguna is clean, efficient and a good way of avoiding traffic. Services tend to run on time and ticket prices start at €1.35 for a single journey. See www.metrotenerife.com for timetables.

Ferry services: Fred Olsen jetfoil takes one hour to Agaete on Gran Canaria from Santa Cruz, where there is a free connecting bus to Las Palmas, taking another hour. Fred Olsen also serves the islands of La Gomera, La Palma, Gran Canaria, Fuerteventura and Lanzarote. Further information from Fred Olsen (www.fredolsen.es). Note that if you have bought your ticket in advance, it must be confirmed at the desk half an hour before departure. Naviera Armas (www.navieraarmas.com) runs ferries from Los Cristianos to La Gomera, La Palma, El Hierro and from Santa Cruz to all the other Canary Islands.

Taxis

The letters SP (*servicio público*) on the front and rear bumpers of a car indicate that it is a taxi; it might also have a green light in the front windscreen or a green sign indicating *'libre'* when it is free. Fixed prices are displayed on a board at the main taxi rank, giving the fares to the most popular destinations. In general, taxis, which are easily found in urban areas, provide an inexpensive method of transport. If in doubt about the price, ask the driver before setting off.

Taxi apps such as Uber are now available in Tenerife, although ride availability tends to be consolidated in the south.

How much is it to *Hotel Mencey*/the town centre? **¿Cuanto es al *Hotel Mencey*/al centro?**

Telephones

Country codes: For the US and Canada dial 1, UK 44, Australia 61, New Zealand 64, the Republic of Ireland 353 and South Africa 27.

Local codes: The code for Spain is +34. For the Canary Islands a prefix must always be dialled, even for local calls: Province of Santa Cruz de Tenerife (Tenerife, El Hierro, La Gomera and La Palma) 922; Province of Las Palmas de Gran Canaria (Gran Canaria, Lanzarote and Fuerteventura) 928.

Time difference

In winter the Canary Islands maintain Greenwich Mean Time, which is one hour behind most European countries, including Spain, but the same as the UK. For the rest of the year the islands go on summertime, as does Spain – keeping the one-hour difference. So, whatever the time is in London, it's the same in Tenerife.

Los Angeles	New York	London	**Canaries**	Madrid
4am	7am	noon	**noon**	1pm

Tipping

Service charge is often included on larger restaurant bills, and tipping is not obligatory. Taxi drivers, bar staff, waiters and hairdressers will appreciate a small tip of a few coins or rounding up the bill by a few euros. Also tip porters and maids a few euros, depending on your length of stay.

Toilets

The most commonly used expressions for toilets in the Canaries are *servicios* or *aseos*, though you may also hear or see WC. Public conveniences are located by most beaches, but otherwise can be difficult to find; where they are available, they are not always the cleanest. Hotels, bars and restaurants usually have lavatories, and it is considered polite to buy a coffee if you do drop in to use their facilities. Accessible toilets for disabled travellers can be difficult to come by outside of large hotels although resorts are becoming much more accessible.

Where are the lavatories? **¿Dónde están los servicios?**

Tourist information

Obtain information on the Canary Islands from www.spain.info or from Spanish National Tourist Offices. The main office for the whole island is the Cabildo Insular in Plaza de España, Santa Cruz de Tenerife. The Tenerife tourist board has two websites: www.webtenerife.com and www.tenerife.es.

Websites

The following websites have useful, up-to-date information about Tenerife:

www.spain.info Spanish tourist office website.

www.hellocanaryislands.com Canary Islands tourism website.

www.webtenerife.com Tourist office site in seven languages.

Index

A

accessible travel 128
accommodation 128
Adeje 83
Aguamansa 65
airports 129
Anaga Hills 47
apps 129
Arguayo 77

B

Bajamar 47
bicycle rental 129
birdwatching 94
Boca de Tauce 69
Bosque la Esperanza 66
budgeting for your trip 130

C

Candelaria 88
car hire 131
Casa del Vino Tenerife 57
Chinamada 49
climate 131
Costa del Silencio 84
crime and safety 131
Cueva del Hermano Pedro 85
customs and entry requirements 132
cycling 92, 129

D

diving 95
driving 132

E

electricity 133
El Médano 84
El Tanque 76
El Teide 61
El Teno Rural Park 70
embassies and consulates 133
emergencies 134
Erjos 76

F

Faro del Teno 74
flora 92
food and drink 107

G

Garachico
  Mirador de Garachico 71
  Plaza de Juan Gonzales de la Torre 72
  Santa Ana church 72
getting to Tenerife 134
golf 94
Granadilla de Abona 86
  Museo de la Historia de Granadilla de Abona 86
Guía de Isora 78
Güímar 87

H

health and medical care 135
hiking 91
horseriding 94

I

Icod de los Vinos 60
  El Drago Milenario 60
  Mariposario del Drago 60
Isla Baja 70

J

jeep tours 92

L

La Caleta 82
La Esperanza 66
La Gomera 83
La Laguna 45
  Ayuntamiento 45, 55
  Convento de Santa Clara 46
  Museo de Antropología de Tenerife 46
  Palacio de Nava 45
  Plaza del Adelantado 45
language 136
La Orotava 55
  Casa de los Balcones 55
  Iglesia de Nuestra Señora de la Concepción 56
  Jardínes Marquesado de la Quinta Roja 55
  San Agustín church 55
Las Galletas 84
La Tejita 84
LGBTQ+ travellers 137
Los Cristianos 82
Los Gigantes 77
Los Organos 66

Los Realejos 59
Los Roques de García 68
lost property 137

M

Marguerita de Piedra 66
Masca 75
Mirador de Don Martín 87
Mirador de El Boquerón 47
Mirador del Pico del Inglés 48
money 137
Montaña del Chinyero 76
Montaña Roja 84
Montañas de Anaga 48
Montañeta del Palmar 75

O

Observatorio Astronómico del Teide 66
Observatorio Atmosférico de Izaña 66
opening hours 138
Orotava Valley 50
outdoor activities 91

P

Parque Etnográfico Pirámides de Güímar 87
Parque Nacional de las Cañadas del Teide 62
Parque Rural de Anaga 48
Playa de las Américas 82
  Baranco del Rey 81
Playa La Caleta de Interián 74
Playa San Marcos 61
Playa San Roque 49
police 138
public holidays 136
public transport 139
Puertito de Güímar 88
Puerto de la Cruz 51
  Ermita de San Juan Batista 51
  Iglesia de Nuestra Señora de la Peña de Francia 52
  Iglesia de San Francisco 52
  Jardín Botánico 54
  promenade 53
Puerto Santiago 77
Punto Hidalgo 47

S

San Cristóbal de la Laguna. See La Laguna
San Juan 78
San Juan de la Rambla 59
Santa Catalina church 58
Santa Cruz
  Cabildo Insular 37
  Calle del Castillo 37
  Iglesia de San Francisco de Asís 38
  Iglesia Matriz de Nuestra Señora de la Concepción 38
  Monumento a los Caídos 36
  Museo de Bellas Artes 38
  Museo de la Naturaleza y el Arqueología 40
  Museo Militar Regional de Canarias 43
  Parque Marítimo César Manrique 42
  Plaza de España 36
  Plaza de la Candelaria 37
  Rambla 43
Santa Cruz de Tenerife 35

T

Tacoronte 58
Tacoronte-Acentejo wine area 57
taxis 140
teleférico 67
Tenerife Honey Centre 58
time difference 140
tipping 141
toilets 141
tourist information 141

V

Vilaflor 68

W

wine 107

MINI
TENERIFE

Second Edition 2025

Editor: Joanna Reeves
Author: Roger Williams
Updater: Ross Clarke
Picture Editor: Piotr Kala
Picture Manager: Tom Smyth
Cartography Update: Katie Bennett
Layout: Claire Armstrong
Production Operations Manager: Katie Bennett
Publishing Technology Manager: Rebeka Davies
Head of Publishing: Sarah Clark
Photography Credits: All images Shutterstock
Cover Credits: El Teide and Roque Cinchado iStock

About the author
Ross Clarke is an award-winning travel, food and wine writer. When he's not island-hopping the Canary or Balearic Islands or traversing mainland Spain in search of great stories, he's exploring the food, culture and history of his homeland of Wales.

Distribution
UK, Ireland and Europe: Apa Publications (UK) Ltd; mail@roughguides.com
United States and Canada: Two Rivers; ips@ingramcontent.com
Australia and New Zealand: Woodslane; info@woodslane.com.au
Worldwide: Apa Publications (UK) Ltd; mail@roughguides.com

MIX
Paper from responsible sources
FSC® C014138

Special Sales, Content Licensing and CoPublishing
Rough Guides can be purchased in bulk quantities at discounted prices. We can create special editions, personalized jackets and corporate imprints tailored to your needs.
mail@roughguides.com
roughguides.com

EU Representative
LOGOS EUROPE, 9 rue Nicolas Poussin, 17000, LA ROCHELLE, France; Contact@logoseurope.eu; +33 (0) 667937378

Printed by Finidr in Czech Republic

ISBN: 9781835292181

This book was produced using **Typefi** automated publishing software.

A catalogue record for this book is available from the British Library

Contact us
Every effort has been made to ensure that this publication is accurate, free from safety risks, and provides accurate information. However, changes and errors are inevitable. The publisher is not responsible for any resulting loss, inconvenience, injury or safety concerns arising from the use of this book. If you notice any errors, outdated information, or potential safety risks, please send your comments with the subject line "Rough Guide Mini Tenerife Update" to mail@roughguides.com.